Your STUDENTS
My STUDENTS
Our STUDENTS

ASCD MEMBER BOOK

Many ASCD members received this book as a
member benefit upon its initial release.

Learn more at: **www.ascd.org/memberbooks**

Your STUDENTS My STUDENTS Our STUDENTS

Rethinking Equitable and Inclusive Classrooms

LEE ANN **JUNG** · NANCY **FREY** · DOUGLAS **FISHER** · JULIE **KROENER**

ASCD | Alexandria, Virginia USA

1703 N. Beauregard St. • Alexandria, VA 22311-1714 USA
Phone: 800-933-2723 or 703-578-9600 • Fax: 703-575-5400
Website: www.ascd.org • E-mail: member@ascd.org
Author guidelines: www.ascd.org/write

Ronn Nozoe, *Interim CEO and Executive Director;* Stefani Roth, *Publisher;* Genny Ostertag, *Director, Content Acquisitions;* Julie Houtz, *Director, Book Editing & Production;* Katie Martin, *Editor;* Judi Connelly, *Senior Art Director;* Thomas Lytle, *Associate Art Director;* Keith Demmons, *Senior Production Designer;* Kelly Marshall, *Interim Manager, Production Services;* Shajuan Martin, *E-Publishing Specialist*

All web links in this book are correct as of the publication date below but may have become inactive or otherwise modified since that time. If you notice a deactivated or changed link, please e-mail books@ascd.org with the words "Link Update" in the subject line. In your message, please specify the web link, the book title, and the page number on which the link appears.

PAPERBACK ISBN: 978-1-4166-2809-5   ASCD product #119019
PDF E-BOOK ISBN: 978-1-4166-2811-8; see Books in Print for other formats.
Quantity discounts are available: e-mail programteam@ascd.org or call 800-933-2723, ext. 5773, or 703-575-5773. For desk copies, go to www.ascd.org/deskcopy.

ASCD Member Book No. FY20-1A (Sep. PSI+). ASCD Member Books mail to Premium (P), Select (S), and Institutional Plus (I+) members on this schedule: Jan, PSI+; Feb, P; Apr, PSI+; May, P; Jul, PSI+; Aug, P; Sep, PSI+; Nov, PSI+; Dec, P. For current details on membership, see www.ascd.org/membership.

Library of Congress Cataloging-in-Publication Data

Names: Jung, Lee Ann, author.
Title: Your students, my students, our students : rethinking equitable and
    inclusive classrooms / Lee Ann Jung, Nancy Frey, Douglas Fisher, Julie
    Kroener.
Description: Alexandria, Virginia : ASCD, [2019] | Includes bibliographical
    references and index.
Identifiers: LCCN 2019021185 (print) | LCCN 2019981192 (ebook) | ISBN
    9781416628095 (paperback) | ISBN 9781416628118 (pdf)
Subjects: LCSH: Inclusive education.
Classification: LCC LC1200 .J88 2019 (print) | LCC LC1200 (ebook) | DDC
    371.9/046—dc23
LC record available at https://lccn.loc.gov/2019021185
LC ebook record available at https://lccn.loc.gov/2019981192

28 27 26 25 24 23 22 21 20 19   1 2 3 4 5 6 7 8 9 10 11 12

Your Students My Students Our Students

Introduction

"Special education class is the place they make you go to do the things you're not good at all day long."

These words of wisdom were spoken by Kevin, a middle school student with autism* who spent most of his school day in a segregated classroom for students with significant disabilities. When overwhelmed, Kevin sometimes exhibited behaviors like hand flapping and rocking. He presented as a child with low communication skills, but he actually had a lot to say.

One day, when Kevin and his older brother were waiting on a corner after school, his brother was struck by gunfire, sustaining relatively minor injuries. However, there is nothing "minor" about getting shot, and the incident left the entire family traumatized. Kevin's parents wanted to move their children to another school within the district, away from the scene of the incident. But Kevin's disability was a sticking point. His mom and dad were distressed by the regression their son had experienced in the wake of his brother's shooting, and they wanted to ensure he had the best opportunities possible. Would it be better for him to stay where he

---

*This diagnosis is formally known as autism spectrum disorder (ASD), but we will use *autism* for brevity and to avoid the term "disorder."

was, with no disruption of service? What other options were available to him in other district schools?

Seeking answers, Kevin's parents attended workshops sponsored by the state parent training and resource center. There, they learned about a new possibility for Kevin: that he might be educated in a general education classroom. As luck would have it, the district was piloting schoolwide inclusive education practices at one middle school and one high school as part of a research study. The boys transferred to these schools. Kevin left his traditional "special education" behind, and this change transformed his life.

Kevin no longer spent his days compelled to do things he wasn't good at all day long. Yes, he required a bit of support in general education courses, but the study project plan spelled out systems for responding to the academic, behavioral, and social needs of all enrolled students. For example, when Kevin's individualized education program (IEP) team noticed that he did not participate in any extracurricular activities, they created goals for him that included attending a dance and a football game and joining an after-school club. Kevin later remarked, "When did the school teach everyone else to go to these things? How come I never learned to make friends?"

Kevin thrived in his new environment. During the summer before his junior year in high school, he earned an enviable amount of money debugging software for a local tech firm. After graduating from high school with honors, he earned an undergraduate degree in engineering and went on to work for a company that—like Microsoft, JPMorgan Chase, and Walgreens—prioritizes hiring people with autism. As enterprise application software company SAP's Silvio Bessa has noted, corporations recruit people with autism because they need the "analytic mindset" that allows them to collectively "think outside of the common boundaries" (SAP, 2013).

Today, Kevin proudly identifies himself as a person with autism and says that he "works well with NTs" (*neurotypicals,* a neologism for people without autism) and appreciates "what they have to offer, too." His inclusive workplace is an extension of the inclusive schooling he was first introduced to in middle school. The world experiences Kevin as a fully integrated member of society. He pays taxes, gets stuck in traffic jams, laments the losses suffered by his favorite sports team, and wishes his romantic life were better. In other words, Kevin is pretty much like everyone else. Yet he is also himself. He has autism, engages in some repetitive behaviors when he is feeling stressed, and sometimes struggles with communicating with colleagues in the workplace. The difference is that he is in a professional community that seeks to understand his differences while never overlooking the human condition that binds us all together.

Where We Are and Where Our Schools Aren't (Yet)

Globalization has flattened our world, and it's also supported greater accessibility to information and services. As one simple example, look at the accessibility features available on your smartphone. You can change the font size and alter colors to make the contrast sharper and therefore easier to read. There is voice recognition software that allows you to text and search without typing out words. Voicemail messages can be read through transcription. These and other innovations reflect the sensibility that "design is a way in which we can uphold a person's dignity and human rights" (Burke, 2017). They grew from the intersection of people with *and* without disabilities participating together in the social and physical world.

And yet school remains a place where these intersections are systematically minimized. This is the result of 200 years of viewing disability through a medical model that catalogs impairment rather than considers disability as a social construct that is shaped by policy, theory, and ethics. It's impossible to untangle disability from race, culture, and economics, and equity cannot be realized if some members of society—and members of school communities—are marginalized and segregated. As a retired superintendent who oversaw the shift to inclusive education practices in his school district would remind his principals, "Show me your master schedule, and I'll tell you what your values are." Who within a building has and does not have access to "regular classes" is often a reflection of who and what matters to the educators who work there.

If students with disabilities and their peers without disabilities are to achieve at higher levels, increase the satisfaction they experience in life, and contribute as members of the community, the education system needs to change—and this will be no easy task. It requires undoing the marginalization of people with disabilities that dates back centuries and changing the expectations for students with disabilities. Yet we must try. The current system is not working for many students, and that's a problem we cannot ignore.

Understanding the Human Experience

Disability is part of the human experience. Once viewed as a static binary construct (disabled/not disabled), disability is now understood as a dimension of a person's identity, alongside race, ethnicity, language, gender, sexual orientation, and experience. It is the intersection of these "identity influences" that make each of us who we are. To segregate students according to a single identity influence—disability—is to sentence them to a "literal disenfranchisement" that marginalizes and threatens their identify as citizens of the world (Kliewer, Biklen, & Kasa-Hendrickson, 2006, p. 186).

Further, the practice of setting up separate classrooms and schools for the education of students with disabilities also limits the experiences of students without disabilities. Consider that about 10 percent of the student population has a disability. This means an equal percentage of families—10 percent—have the experience of either rearing or growing up with a child who has a disability. What does that mean for the 90 percent of students and families—the future employers, co-workers, landlords, neighbors, medical professionals, law enforcement officers, teachers, and parents—who may not have opportunities to spend time around people with a disability and get to know them as individuals with personalities, quirks, challenges, and successes? It's not an overstatement to say that society would be changed for the better if every school child had the chance to know and learn alongside people with disabilities and see them as peers. It's not about pity; it's about the recognition of fundamental rights and human dignity.

The good news is that there are places where inclusive education is happening. These schools are populated by teachers and leaders who recognize that students with disabilities are rightfully part of general education classrooms. They are working relentlessly to align supports and services with the students' needs and, in so doing, ensure that every single student has a full and powerful learning experience. These schools and systems are models of success, and they can be a guide for undertaking widespread change.

Characteristics of Successful Inclusive Practice

American teachers often assume that the United States leads the world in special education, largely because of the decades-old legislation mandating that students with disabilities be served by public schools. But many other countries have also been successfully including students with disabilities for decades. Take, for example, Italy's approach to inclusion, which departs from the U.S. system in several important ways. In their study of Italian schools, Giangreco and Doyle (2015) describe four fundamental attributes that distinguish inclusive efforts in Italian schools from those in the United States. Let's look at them one at a time.

A Universally Welcoming Environment

It's widely acknowledged that open and welcoming environments lead to engaged students and families, and that increased engagement yields better long-term outcomes for students. We have yet to meet teachers who don't aspire to be inviting and welcoming to students and their families. But for families of students with disabilities in the United States, the reality does not always match the espoused aspiration. Too many parents find they must advocate for their children to be included or adequately served in general education classrooms. Students with significant disabilities are too frequently served in segregated settings for part or even all of the school day. More than 20 percent of students with multiple disabilities are educated in segregated environments (National Center for Education Statistics, 2017).

By contrast, the norm in Italian schools is that students of all levels of ability, including those with significant disabilities, spend their full day in general education classrooms. According to Giangreco and Doyle (2015), Italians are often shocked to hear that many students with disabilities in the United States are denied access to the general education classroom and only receive services in special education classrooms. They add, "For the most part, including students with disabilities in Italy is not controversial, an experiment, a passing fad, or a right that needs to be earned by meeting certain criteria or functioning at a particular level. Students with disabilities are welcomed simply because they are human" (p. 26).

A Narrow Definition of *Disability*

Giangreco and Doyle point out that the Italian category "disability" applies only to students with more significant needs. What the United States would diagnose as *learning disability*, for example, is not seen as a disability in Italy; it's simply part of the range that any general education teacher is expected to support. In the United States, 10 to 15 percent of students in a typical school qualify for special education services, which they receive on the basis of their individualized education plans (IEPs). But in Italy, only 2 to 3 percent of students are identified as having a disability for which they require specialized supports. Most of the students in the United States with IEPs would not be considered to have a disability in Italy; they would simply fall into Italian education's broader scope of "normal." Italian laws do require that students who have learning needs receive appropriate accommodations, but no student needs to have a disability label to receive this support.

General Education Ownership of All Students

Given the narrower definition of disability in Italy, it is not surprising that general education teachers have a sense of ownership for the learning of all students in their classroom, including those who, in the United States, might be identified as having multiple or severe disabilities. In U.S. classrooms, students with more significant disabilities almost always have additional support in the classroom, usually assigned to the student. Most U.S. students with significant disabilities also spend part or all of their day at school in segregated, special education classrooms (National Center for Education Statistics, 2017).

By contrast, few "special education classrooms" exist in Italian schools. The presence of students with learning needs is expected in general education classroom, meaning "pullout" services are rare. Italian general and special education teachers collaborate and develop solutions for educating all students in the same classroom. Additional support is available to many general education classrooms, but only for part of the day or week. Both the general education teacher and special education teacher or paraprofessional support all students, not an assigned subset.

Less Reliance on Paraprofessionals

In the United States, there is an increasing reliance on paraprofessionals to provide instruction to students with disabilities, with families and teachers commonly making the case for one-on-one assistants attached to individual students (Giangreco, 2013). Often seen as a cost-effective way to get individualized support to more students, paraprofessionals are charged with supporting instruction, oftentimes beyond the scope of what they have been trained and prepared to do. Italian schools, on the other hand, rely very little on paraprofessionals, and the paraprofessional's role is largely to provide assistance with feeding, toileting, and mobility within the classroom and around the school; it is not instruction. Italian schools view the design of intervention and supports as the responsibility of the general and special education teachers.

Transforming Inclusive Education to Serve Every Student

In a team-based model of inclusive education, all students receive the benefit of support within the general education classroom setting. The full scope of this approach's benefits may be impossible to measure fully. Consider that because true inclusion elevates teaching practices in general education classrooms, many students will likely never need "supplemental" instruction or intervention. Students who might have been identified as at risk for school failure under older models will succeed without intervention and never be stigmatized, labeled, or *othered*.

Benefits for Students Needing Support

Decades of special education studies have demonstrated that students who are taught in inclusive settings show higher achievement than those who are pulled from the general education classroom (Cole, Waldron, & Majd, 2004; Manset & Semmel, 1997; Rea, McLaughlin, & Walther-Thomas, 2002; Westling & Fox, 2009). Students with learning differences who are served in inclusive settings are also more likely to pursue post-secondary education (Baer et al., 2003; Flexer, Daviso, Baer, Queen, & Meindl, 2011; Joshi & Bouck, 2017; Lombardi, Doren, Gau, & Lindstrom, 2013; Rojewski, Lee, & Gregg, 2013). Inclusion's benefits to students with learning differences, however, extend beyond academic achievement. Inclusive service delivery also leads to higher social and communication outcomes for students (Calabrese et al., 2008; Foreman, Arthur-Kelly, Pascoe, King, & Downing, 2004; Katz, Mirenda, & Auerbach, 2002).

Stories like Kevin's appeal to our sense of human rights and social justice. The right to be included should have been sufficient to ensure that Kevin participated fully in his schooling from the very beginning. But what drives us—and you—is figuring out effective ways to support all students. We maintain that supporting students with a wide variety of learning profiles in the general education classroom is good *for everyone,* and research backs this view. Szumski, Smogorzewska, and Karwowski (2017) performed a meta-analysis of 47 studies examining the effect of inclusive education on students without disabilities. The almost 5 million students from seven countries—including the United States and Canada—did not have disabilities but were educated in inclusive classrooms. The researchers found a small but positive effect on the academic and social growth of these students. In their conclusion, the researchers made this statement:

> This result may be important to educational policymakers responsible for decisions about the promotion of inclusion, but also to parents of children without [special educational needs]. Even more importantly, the main effect of this meta-analysis supplements and supports argumentation in favor of promoting inclusion. . . . The effects we obtained—both the main effect and the results of moderator analysis—consistently support the concept of inclusive education, understood as effective school for all. (p. 47)

Benefits for Educators and Other Professionals

Szumski and colleagues also describe inclusive education as a vehicle for "a radical concept of educational system transformation" (p. 47). The desired outcome, of course, is ensuring access and high achievement for all students. One of the reasons inclusion works so well for everyone is that it elevates the quality of instruction in the general education classroom. When general education teachers have a broader range of learning profiles in their classrooms, they have to adapt and gain new strategies to teach each of these students. Some of these new strategies are gained through the teacher's own reflection and examination of classroom-level data. Other strategies are gained through learning from a co-teacher or specialist in the room. Through both routes, the general education teachers become better teachers with more robust practices (Fisher, Sax, Rodifer, & Pumpian, 1999).

Similarly, specialists brought into the general education classrooms as co-teachers gain a deeper understanding of the general curriculum. Skills are no longer a checklist of isolated items; they come alive in the context of the general curriculum and daily school routines. Having this context is essential for effective goal setting and support planning (Fisher & Frey, 2014b).

Your Kids, My Kids, *Our* Kids

The stories of students and teachers in this book are real; we directly experienced each of the situations that we describe. Although we have changed the names of people involved, all of the good, the bad, and the ugly portrayed really happened. The four of us—Lee Ann, Nancy, Doug, and Julie—have a combined 100 years of experience in schools, and we have spent those years working to create educational environments that welcome the full range of human experience.

This book is for school leaders and any educator for whom people with disabilities are people first: family, neighbors, part of the community, and students in the classrooms and hallways of our schools. All educators have a circle of influence in their capacity as professionals, and we hope that you will use yours to work toward creating equitable and inclusive learning environments for all students.

The work of transforming school practices and organization to improve the learning lives of *every student* begins with educators and relies on our ability to increase our own efficacy. Yes, you are likely to encounter some ideas in this book and think, "I can't change that. I'm just one person." Perhaps you aren't in a decision-making role as it applies to some of the programmatic, fiscal, or human resources recommendations we make. But you do have a voice. You can advocate for incremental changes. You can influence one, who can influence others, to spark the change. After all, it was a groundswell of many voices that brought about two monumental pieces of legislation: the desegregation of schools based on race and the mandate that children with disabilities receive a free and appropriate public education. These events fundamentally changed the education landscape in the latter half of the 20th century. Now, well into the 21st century, it is past time to build on these foundational principles.

We see the education of students with disabilities as an equity issue. This book focuses on areas that must receive attention in order to realize the promise of providing a meaningful educational experience for all students, including students with disabilities. Toward that end, we have identified five disruptions to the status quo that are needed to move inclusive schooling practices to the next level—Inclusion 2.0, if you will. These areas of focus build on the work that others have done to open doors for students with disabilities:

- Establish an inclusive culture that champions equity and inclusion (Chapter 1).
- Reimagine the long-standing structure of least restrictive environment and resulting service delivery (Chapter 2).
- Leverage the strengths of all educators to benefit each student (Chapter 3).
- Collaborate on the delivery of instruction and intervention (Chapter 4).
- Honor the aspirations of students and plan accordingly (Chapter 5).

Like you, the four of us are involved in the day-to-day lives of students, families, and teachers. Our work in schools charges us with solving problems. In each chapter of this book, we present solutions to address the issue of building capacity so that each student receives an equitable education. Only by addressing issues of equity for students with disabilities—a historically marginalized group—is it possible to build a system for creating equitable solutions for all students. And it's only by relentlessly pursuing change (the topic of Chapter 6) that we can realize true inclusion.

We hope this introduction has intrigued you to read on. We hope the real stories of discrimination and failure, of empowerment and success, in the pages ahead will appeal to your sense of social justice. Ultimately, we hope that this book will inspire you to take up the charge and advocate for a stronger education system that values the contributions of every member of our society. *Your voice matters.*

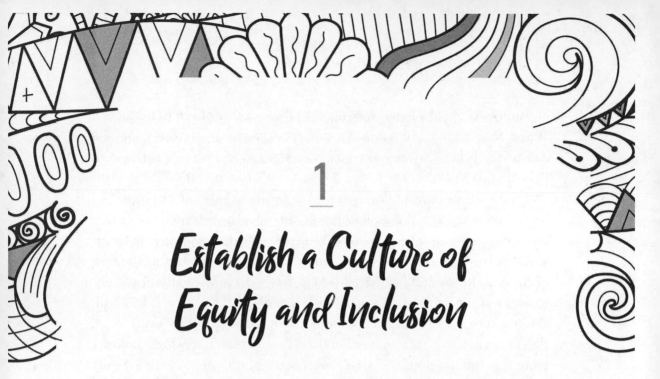

1

Establish a Culture of Equity and Inclusion

Andrew rolls down the hallway of his middle school with two other students walking alongside him. Suddenly Andrew's wheelchair stops, and he looks at his lap tray. Sean and Jesse notice and back up to flank Andrew again. He is pointing to a word on his tray.

"Wait, what did you say?" asks Sean.

Andrew looks at his lap tray again and touches the word *you*.

Jesse repeats it aloud: "You."

Then Andrew moves to the letter area, touching *f*, *o*, *r*, and *g*.

"Forgot?" Jesse offers.

Andrew nods, smiling, and then looks back to his tray, touching *you* and *r*.

Jesse says, "Your."

Andrew starts spelling again: *b*, *o*, *o*, *k*.

Jesse gets it. "Oh man, you're right! I gotta have the book for English. Thanks for reminding me. I'll catch up. Maybe you guys can distract Ms. VanArk so she doesn't notice I'm late!"

Andrew and Sean head off to class while Jesse runs back to his locker. When they get to Ms. VanArk's classroom, Sean opens the door and Andrew rolls in. Sean moves a chair that is blocking Andrew's path, probably mistakenly left there by the last group of students. It's all very ordinary, and no one seems to notice the give-and-take between the boys.

In another part of the building, a group of teachers is meeting during planning time and working through a series of learning progressions for a unit of study on the American Revolution. They are discussing the flow of the daily lessons and which materials they want to use to build student mastery of the content. Teacher Brad Henderson says, "In our last unit, I'm not sure we had students reading enough from primary sources. I'd like to see our students do more of that. There are so many great sources from this time period. We could select some and then have them ready in large print, audio, and adapted versions. I would like to use them in small groups this time so that I can see how students are responding to the texts."

There is general agreement. Then teacher Amal Ali says, "Before we go any further, can we revisit the assessments we'll use? I've been thinking about it, and we need to give students more choices for how they can demonstrate mastery. And I think they all should have practice with a formal assessment and options for how to demonstrate understanding in creative ways. Thoughts?"

The team continues discussing their plans and building an inclusive set of experiences for students. They do not talk about "what to do about SPED students" or how to adjust developed lessons to accommodate specific learning needs—the sort of conversation that is prevalent in many schools. It's not even clear which of the teachers are "special educators" and which are "general educators." What *is* clear is that all of the teachers present value the learning of all students in much the same way that Andrew, Sean, and Jesse value each other—casually, as an ordinary matter of course. This way of regarding all students as "our students" is far from common. But that could change, and it needs to.

Beliefs Drive Inclusive Education and Equity

We start with the culture of inclusion because it's foundational to the creation of schools that work for all students. The philosophy of the staff within a school directly and significantly affects the systems of support that are available for students. We have learned the hard way that meaningful improvements in what a school *does* only stick and have purpose when the adults in the school reevaluate what they know and come to a new understanding of the labels and language they use, how instruction and intervention should be delivered, where students are served, the roles of everyone in the school, and what their expectations are—for both their students and themselves.

Shanice's family moved to a new city the summer before she started high school. The first 10 years of her school experience were spent in self-contained special education classrooms with no participation at all in the general education classroom. During elementary school, she and the other students with disabilities even ate lunch at a different time than the rest of the student body. They were different, a group apart.

At Shanice's new school, all of her classes were general education courses: Earth Science, English 9, Algebra I, Art, and Biology. When Shanice's mother called at the end of the second week and asked to meet with the principal and special education teacher, they worried that something was wrong. In fact, when they sat down to meet with Shanice's mom, the first question they asked her was, "Is everything OK?"

Shanice's mom started to cry. It took her several minutes to compose herself, and when she did, this is what she said:

> It's like you gave me a different kid. She has grown so much in academics and social skills. I can't believe that I agreed to keeping her out of regular classes all those years. I'm glad I trusted you this summer when we met and you said that your philosophy was that students belonged together and that you could

organize supports. I let you try, but really, I was expecting you to call and tell me that it wasn't working. But you didn't, because it is. Thank you for all that you're doing for my daughter.

Did Shanice's needs suddenly change over the summer? Or did Shanice change in response to her new experiences in a school committed to the belief that all students had the capacity to meet high expectations and committed to maintaining systems of support to align with that belief? We, and the actual parties involved, know it was the latter. Shanice became different because the new school she went to was different. It was more sophisticated, and the members of the staff valued the membership of all students and had figured out how to support students' various needs. We have never encountered an inclusive school in which the faculty did not believe in what they were doing. As you will see over and over again in this book, it's the philosophy that drives an effective system.

With the rapid growth in programs to support students who are struggling, it can be tempting to latch onto one of those as a starting point. School leaders may, for example, attempt to nudge the needle of inclusion by launching a full-tilt multi-tiered system of supports (MTSS) effort, implementing a reading intervention program, or digging into a complete overhaul of their individualized education program (IEP) process. While these are essential components of successfully inclusive schools, starting with procedures rather than with the vision dooms a school to a series of never-ending "tweaks" and a seemingly infinite number of "initiatives." Achieving the outcome students deserve requires a complete reimagining. Equity and inclusion must become the ethos of the school. Excellent education for all should be the objective and the impetus—what drives every initiative, program, or strategy.

Shifting the culture of a school to embrace inclusion is much more complicated than simply sharing the research that says inclusion works (e.g., Fisher, Roach, & Frey, 2002). It involves dismantling the status quo, disrupting long-held beliefs about learners and about teaching.

Fundamental to this work is replacing a climate of *sorting and ranking* students with one of *mastery*—believing and expecting that all students can achieve at high levels.

Having a culture of mastery means every single person in the school embraces every student, without exception, as worthy and deserving of their best. It means never turning our back on a student because "she's yours, not mine." It means never giving up on *any* student, because there's an expectation that *every* student can achieve at a higher level than ever before. In a culture of mastery, everyone on staff believes that in order to meet the needs of *all* students, it's necessary to meet the needs of *each* student.

Language and Labels Matter

If excellent educational outcomes for all is the goal (it is), the sobering truth is that there is a long way to go. Regardless of whether the measure is achievement scores, graduation rates, post-school employment, or college acceptance rates, the conclusion is the same: students with disabilities are not faring well in the current education system.

These poor outcomes are fueled in part by the damage done when disability labeling lowers expectations. Students identified as having disabilities encounter bias from their teachers, especially in the form of lower expectations, more negative evaluation of behavior, and negative predictions about whether they are likely to earn an undergraduate degree (Shifrer, 2013). And this culture affects all marginalized students, not only those with disabilities. Because of the evolution of essentially separate systems, special education has long been used as a way to label and segregate instead of support. The dichotomous sorting of our education system has led to inappropriately labeling a disproportionate number of African American students, particularly boys, as having behavioral disorders (Cooc & Kiru, 2018). The majority of U.S. school systems are staffed by adults who are largely white, female, and middle class, and they can struggle to understand behavior expression unlike their own (Delpit, 2006). Most often, the problem isn't even students' behavior per se; it's the mismatch in cultural expectations and a misunderstanding of high- and low-context behaviors.

When Hattie (2012) used meta-analyses from 50,000 studies to calculate the magnitude of 250 different influences on student achievement, he determined that the overall effect size (the magnitude of an influence) equivalent to a year's worth of academic growth in school is .40. The practice of not labeling students (e.g., as "struggling," "gifted," "high achieving," "special ed") has an effect size of .61, meaning that it accelerates learning. Although it is necessary to identify whether a student qualifies for an IEP in order to receive special education services and safeguards, in the daily classroom, labeling has a negative effect. The label often becomes "the reason" why the student is not progressing. Students develop low expectations for themselves, because that's what everyone else does, and the self-fulfilling prophecy is realized when students meet these low expectations. Kirby (2017) notes that the combination of poor self-concept and negative views of teachers has a lasting effect on students, which is counter to the mission of educators. As he puts it, "The education system should be decreasing the impact of disability on a student's academic performance, not exacerbating it" (p. 183). In short, labeling can too easily marginalize and hurt rather than help.

The practice of "tracking" students, common in the 1970s and 1980s, illustrates exactly the harm that results from leaving student needs unmet. As early as kindergarten, students were sorted into ability groups based on their academic performance and perceived potential (low, medium, and high). The idea was to provide greater academic challenges for students who were ready to move forward and greater support to those who struggled. In actuality, though, students in the lower groups received slower-paced instruction as a *replacement* for core instruction—which effectively trapped them within their track throughout their elementary and secondary years. They sank further and further behind, and by high school, many of these students were grade levels behind in crucial literacy, problem-solving, and mathematics skills. This service delivery model failed students who could have been college- and career-bound by not providing them with simple interventions in early childhood. For students with disabilities, the situation was even worse: they were tracked into segregated special education classrooms with an even weaker curriculum.

Unfortunately, tracking lives on. There are still permanent ability groups of low-, middle-, and high-achieving students in some elementary classrooms. Students remain homogenously grouped with similarly achieving students throughout the day. The low-achieving groups are especially vulnerable, as they lack the language, social, and academic models that are present in heterogeneous groups. Although needs-based small-group instruction is an effective practice, permanent ability grouping and tracking have a detrimental effect on students' self-efficacy and on their level of school engagement (Dumont, Protsch, Jansen, & Becker, 2017).

Changing the culture of a school to be receptive to real inclusion starts with changing the language educators use. First, labels belong in the conversation only when discussing services and rights; they have no place in a conversation about the systems of support for a student. Second, in times when it's necessary to speak of disability categories or supports, all faculty should feel the importance of, and embrace the use of, people-first language. Rather than "autistic child," say "a child with autism" (when talking about services and supports)—or just call the kid by his name: Timothy. Rather than say Angela is "wheelchair-bound," you might mention that Angela "rolls to class." Changes in language serve as the foundation for the widespread change in mindset that must occur if schools are ever to deliver on the promise of equity for all students, including those with disabilities.

Not only is there a history of the overuse of disability labels, but too many schools have also acquired the habit of labeling students based on the supports they need: "Let's have a meeting about our Tier 2s and 3s this afternoon." There are no "special education students" or "Tier 2" or "Tier 3 students," and students are never exclusively "yours" or "mine." Every student in the building is *our student* first and foremost. Special education and Tier 2 and 3 interventions are supports that are provided. They are nouns, not adjectives, and they should never be used to describe a student's permanent or long-term status. They are not any student's identity.

What's more, all students in the building are on the specialist's or special educator's caseload. Any child who can benefit from a specialized strategy, accommodation, or modification is their responsibility. And do you know of any student who has never needed support with *anything* academically, socially, or otherwise during their formative years? To deny expert assistance to a student in need because there is no IEP in place is to deny that student an equitable education.

Everyone Deserves to Belong

The 1970s also introduced the practice of *mainstreaming*—an early attempt to create less restrictive placements for students with mild disabilities. In this model, students who demonstrated competence could receive their education in the general education classroom. But this approach placed the burden on students: they had to somehow catch up to grade level while receiving a lower-level replacement curriculum, and then they had to maintain progress in the general education setting. In other words, these students had to continuously prove they "belonged." As problematic as this was for students with mild disabilities, it proved to be even more discouraging for students with significant disabilities.

This "prove you belong" mindset persists. During one IEP meeting Julie attended, a therapist said, "When Justine develops some of her daily living skills—like toothbrushing and feeding herself—she might be able to spend some time in general education." In this therapist's mind, membership in the 4th grade class was dependent on personal care. Doug attended an IEP meeting during which a special educator said, "Once Brad has mastered 100 sight words, he can probably go to the regular class." Does mastery of any number of sight words predict success in the general education classroom? And what better place for Brad to learn sight words than alongside his peers, who already know them? Reading instruction does not stop or start at sight words, and the instruction necessary for all aspects of reading can be provided in the general education classroom. Students with disabilities in general education classrooms deserve the supports and services their IEP teams have designed. In addition, general and special educators deserve to teach in environments engineered so that students can perform at high levels.

In many schools, the default for students with disabilities is still to either put them into the lowest track in general education or assign them to a segregated special education classroom. Although this could technically provide access to grade-level curriculum, too often the special education class is taught by someone who does not have deep content knowledge, and thus, expectations are lowered. We visited a high school in which the special education teacher was expected to teach three different history classes (World History, U.S. History, and Government) in the same period to different students. And the special education teacher had neither a history degree nor credentials in that area.

The long-term outcomes for this practice are dismal. The gaps in learning that persist are evidence that teaching students below-grade-level content is not working. The model of "pull out and *replace* the curriculum" isn't effective for students who need support. The approach that works is an inclusive one in which students receive the general education instruction *and* supplemental instruction (Fuchs et al., 2006; Torgesen, 2002).

A Culture of Intervention for *All*

The inception of special education legislation in 1975 established, via funding mechanisms, the practice of sorting students into two groups:

those who have a defined disability and those who do not. Ever since, the "disability" label has determined whether students qualify for an IEP, special education services, and the legal protections of the Individuals with Disabilities Education Act (IDEA, 2006).

For example, a student could receive an intellectual disability diagnosis by scoring at least two standard deviations below the mean on a standardized test of intellectual functioning. A student with an IQ score of 70 or below would be eligible for intellectual disability diagnosis and thus qualify for and receive special education services and support. A student with an IQ score of 72 would not be eligible for the diagnosis, the services, or the support. There is no grey area in this model; students are "in" and get support, or they are "out" and don't.

Of course, narrowly missing the test range doesn't mean that a student's academic struggles will suddenly disappear. What about the student who "narrowly misses" the definition of *autism?* Or *learning disability?* Or any other disability? The truth is that the students we serve are on a continuum, and while some will formally qualify for special education supports and services, others will not—and yet, these students still have needs to be met.

While this overly simplified sorting strategy may meet the technical definition of providing students with disabilities access to the general curriculum, it has little to do with addressing the core question: *What do students actually need to be successful in the general curriculum?* Some students who need intensive support do not meet the criteria for a disability label. And many students who have a disability label do not need intensive support. The definitions are simply a way to identify some students and provide them with, as Snow (2005) says, "a sociopolitical passport to services" (p. 2).

It's essential to remember that a student's disability status is not the same as a student's needs, and the two should not be confused. *Disability status* is a means for schools to assign fiscal and personnel assets. A student's *need for support* may not result in a formal designation or paperwork such as an IEP, but those needs are also met through fiscal assets in the form of personnel, curriculum, and technology. Think of it this way: a student who needs intensive intervention to learn to read fluently should be provided that intensive intervention. It doesn't matter if the student isn't reading fluently because of a learning disability, because English is a second language, because past years' reading instruction was dreadful, or because of frequent absences. It doesn't matter if no reason is ever identified at all. The student has a need, and it's the school's responsibility to provide the support to address it. Disability labels are largely irrelevant to everyday teaching because they tell us so little about what individual students need; there isn't "autism math" or "physical disability reading." By removing a focus on labels, we can concentrate on the important work of planning and providing meaningful instruction for each student. Students who have disabilities do not have "special needs"; they only have special *rights*. And any student who has a need, with or without a disability, may benefit from the expertise of a specialist.

Accommodations and Modifications for Every Student

Disability status doesn't inform instruction; it should not be the sole criterion when making decisions about providing accommodations and modifications. If students need support to succeed, it should not matter whether they have been identified as having a disability. If a child needs help, why would we not provide it?

Issues of fairness are often raised in response to this question. Maybe you've heard, "It's not fair to give a student extra time on this test unless they have a documented disability." But think about where the lack of fairness *really* lies. Taking a close look at what accommodations and modifications actually accomplish, it becomes clear that these are simply necessary strategies to help students learn. In other words, they are part of the equity efforts schools use to ensure that all students ultimately succeed. Just as the expertise of specialists can benefit all students, truly inclusive environments ensure that accommodations and modifications are available for *any* student who needs them.

Accommodations

Accommodations (see Figure 1.1) are changes to the curriculum or assessments that provide access to the general curriculum but do not fundamentally alter the learning goal or grade-level standard. These supports

Figure 1.1

TYPES OF ACCOMMODATIONS

Type	Definition	Examples
Size	Reduces the number of items a student must complete, with no change to difficulty	• The student is assigned 10 multiplication problems rather than 20, but the difficulty of problems is not altered.
Time	Adjusts amount of time allotted for learning, task completion, or testing	• The student is allowed extra time to complete a test.
Input	Specifies the way instruction is delivered to the learner	• The student gets guided notes to use in Earth Science.
Output	Specifies how the learner can respond to instruction	• The student creates a poster instead of writing a research paper for World History. • The student dictates answers to worksheet questions about addition facts.
Level of support	Identifies the amount of personal assistance to an individual learner	• The student uses a LiveScribe pen to record a conversation with a teacher for later use in writing. • A peer helps the student with the physical construction of a diorama of the first mission in California.

"level the playing field" (Freedman, 2005, p. 47). Put another way, accommodations are *support for a skill that is different from the skill being taught and assessed* (Jung, 2018a). Take, for example, a student learning to drive. The skill being taught and measured is driving. If the student is nearsighted and needs glasses during driving instruction and during the driver's exam in order to read street signs and see other vehicles more clearly, wearing glasses is an accommodation. It makes mastering the skill of driving easier, but it doesn't make it easier than it would be for anyone else; the accommodation simply levels the playing field. And it does not matter if a person who wears glasses does not fit into a disability category; the accommodation is provided any time it is needed. In fact, if a person needs glasses, driving skills cannot be measured with validity if the glasses are not allowed. Putting fairness aside, this is a basic measurement issue.

The same applies to academic content. Consider a social studies class where the purpose of a lesson is to teach students to evaluate the credibility of sources. At present, Akemi, a student who is an English learner, is much better at expressing what she knows verbally than in writing. So the social studies teacher, Ms. Kintzler, allows Akemi to complete the lesson task orally instead of in writing. The teacher sits with Akemi and asks her to describe how she evaluated the sources of evidence for credibility. Ms. Kintzler asks follow-up questions, as do two other students who are included in the conversation because Ms. Kintzler believes exposure to Akemi's explanation will help them strengthen their own written responses. The content of Akemi's responses is evaluated as any other student's response is evaluated, against the same requirements or standards. It's an accommodation made to allow for valid measurement.

There are likely several students in any class that would benefit from these types of supports. One key to meeting the various needs in a classroom is to mobilize peers. Collaborative learning allows students to engage in meaningful tasks while the teacher meets with individuals or small groups. In addition, peers can provide support to members of their class.

In Ms. Kintzler's social studies class, some students with test anxiety need additional time or a separate setting when undergoing assessments. The teacher also reads questions or prompts for one student who has significant difficulty with reading. These basic adaptations are accommodations because they support skills that are *different* from the social studies standards being taught and measured. And, just like wearing glasses while driving, it doesn't matter whether a student fits into a disability category; the accommodation should be provided any time it is needed. Accommodations do not make the content easier; they *permit access* to it. Again, this is a measurement issue: without providing these students these accommodations, Ms. Kintzler would be unable to measure the students' skills in social studies because the expression of those skills is affected by an outside influence (e.g., test anxiety, reading difficulty, writing difficulty). Disability status is irrelevant here; all Ms. Kintzler needs to know when designing and implementing accommodations is that there is an issue, separate from an understanding of the social studies content, that prevents her students from being able to show what they know or are able to do.

Modifications

Modifications (see Figure 1.2) function differently from accommodations; they are changes to the curriculum and assessments that *do* fundamentally alter the learning goal or grade-level expectation. Unlike accommodations, which simply level the playing field, modifications "change the game" (Freedman, 2005, p. 48) and support the skill that is being taught and measured (Jung, 2017b). Returning to the vision example, if a person wears glasses or contact lenses during an eye exam, this changes what is being measured. In reporting the results of any assessment with modifications, it is important to record the modification provided, because something different was being measured. In this example, the optician might be measuring the effectiveness of the contact lens prescription.

Figure 1.2
SAMPLE MODIFICATIONS

Type	Definition	Examples
Same only less	The number of items is reduced or content is adapted to change the level of difficulty or complexity	• The student chooses between two possible answers on a multiple-choice quiz rather than five. • The student's timed fluency measure is shortened to meet the student's developmental level. • The student is assigned a book at a lower reading level.
Streamline the curriculum	The assignment is reduced in breadth or focus to emphasize the key points	• In English, the student creates a list of main points instead of writing an essay. • The teacher simplifies vocabulary for a social studies unit.
Same activity with infused objective	The activity emphasizes IEP objectives or skills from the infused skills grid	• The student answers yes/no questions using his eyes to locate words on his lap tray; teachers and classmates phrase questions in this format.

Suppose students in a class are working on algebra problems that require multiplication of fractions. Erik needs support. He is working below grade level in math and is learning multiplication with whole numbers. Erik's practice work and assessments do not include the grade-level algebraic problems that require multiplication of fractions. Instead, he is practicing with whole-number multiplication problems and one-step algebra problems requiring addition and subtraction. This is a comparably rigorous skill for this student; the adapted skill is just as difficult for this student as the grade-level skill is for students who do not need support. What is being taught and measured has been changed, however, and the math skill being assessed is the skill that is being supported.

It is important to clearly record when a student's progress is based on modified expectations. Making modifications to assignments or other tasks and reporting the student's performance without acknowledging the modification sends the message that the student is performing at grade level. Teachers should always aim for accurate communication regarding how students are performing.

It is also essential to note that modifications should be provided any time they are needed, but not unnecessarily. As we like to say, *only as "special" as necessary*. Modifications change what is expected of the student, in effect saying, "This student is not currently on track to master the grade-level expectation. We are putting into place a comparably rigorous modified expectation." This is serious business, and modifications should be used only when absolutely necessary—and this should be a team decision, supported by data on the student's performance in the context of high-quality instruction and intervention. Teachers also need to be on guard against providing "accidental modifications" through well-meaning support. A teacher might not go so far as to formally modify expectations for a student, but sometimes cueing and scaffolding and prompting and hinting result in providing an accidental modification.

The Power of Expectations

The voicing of low expectations for students with disabilities and their families often starts very early in their lives. Lee Ann's friend Susan has a daughter named Irene who was born with a rare genetic condition called chromosome 5p deletion syndrome. The medical team told Susan and her husband that Irene would never walk, talk, or be able to go to school.

A kid named Alfredo shared in a transition planning meeting that after he was diagnosed with attention deficit hyperactivity disorder, his mother was told by members of his special education team that he would "never be successful in life" and that he would never do well in school. They told her that he would never graduate from high school or be able to hold a job. His mother was devastated, and who wouldn't be?

With any diagnosis, it's impossible to know exactly what the future will hold. Today, Irene is a healthy, happy, spunky teenager who walks, talks, runs, reads, writes, jokes, laughs, lives a full life, and spends her time at school in the general education classroom. Alfredo went on to graduate from high school with a 3.8 grade point average, and he has completed his first year at a four-year university as a criminal justice major. Some might say Irene is a miracle. Perhaps it is a medical marvel that she is healthy and has the physical abilities that she does, but it is no miracle that she is achieving her potential. Her entire family has worked very hard to make sure Irene's dreams were realized. Similarly, Alfredo's mother decided that she wouldn't let her son's disability define him; she focused on possibilities and ensured that others on Alfredo's educational team did the same. This is what happens when we have high expectations and put supports in place to ensure students have every chance to reach them.

Too often, students and their families run into the wall of low and limited expectations. Educators should be very careful about predicting the future. We have no idea what the future holds, what innovations and inventions will come, and how students will respond to great learning experiences. The least dangerous assumption we can make is that students will learn and that they will have amazing lives. The most dangerous assumption we can make is that students will fail. Imagine the difference when our assumptions come true.

When professionals focus on what *can't* happen, they are also putting limitations on a student's ability to dream. The professionals in these stories surely didn't intend to crush children's and parents' dreams. Educators don't go into the field because they want to squash children's aspirations. But in far too many instances, well-meaning physicians, therapists, counselors, psychologists, and educators enter the conversation about a student's future with their own ideas and expectations of how this future should look. Who are we to decide what is or isn't possible for a student? No disability—whether a specific learning disability, physical disability, intellectual disability, or any diagnosis—should limit the future for any individual to have a life of fulfillment, one in which they feel they belong and contribute and receive joy in their everyday lives. This is what every human being deserves.

It is the responsibility of adult mentors to guide young people along the path to success however *those young people* define success. Attending to the aspirations of students and their families is an issue of cultural competence. In this way, educators take on the role of dream manager: paving a path and allowing students to meet their goals. The dream manager validates and supports the dream, no matter how lofty it may seem, identifying and removing obstacles to help make it happen. Haven't we all set what seemed to be unrealistic goals for ourselves? Even when we don't actually reach the goal, more often than not, the setting of the goal and striving to meet these goals causes us to push harder and go for something big. And how often have you surprised yourself in what you can achieve?

Hattie's meta-analyses of numerous educational studies (2012) revealed that students' expectations of their own success are among the greatest predictors of their outcomes, with an effect size of 1.44. Limiting students' ability to dream limits their actual outcomes. Our job as educators is to support the student's vision, hope, and dreams, and *never* get in the way or diminish the possibilities.

Throughout the IEP process, educators are wise to take advantage of families' knowledge and treat them as a full partner at the table. Families are the constant in children's lives and know their children best. This expertise is often overlooked and not used as a cornerstone for developing IEPs and transition plans. Over the course of their elementary and secondary years, children spend a lot of time in school. How are teachers connecting with families in identifying children's aspirations and aligning curriculum and activities to the goals and dreams of each child? When communication with families is strong, educators and parents can share the role of dream manager.

Conclusion

The drive for truly inclusive education is a critical part of the broader effort aimed at achieving equity in education. It means reimagining systems to expand every student's access to both the general education curriculum *and* intervention supports and services. It also means building a culture in which this expansion is the expectation and the norm, in which everyone agrees that there is no such thing as "good teaching" that leaves some students unserved and unsupported.

Creating this new and better model of education begins with taking action to adjust the language used in schools, the services provided, and the expectations set for students with disabilities and those at risk. Doing so establishes a climate in which students can achieve outcomes that might once have been considered unrealistic.

Changing the Culture

THE CHALLENGES

School staff have not examined their beliefs and values related to students with disabilities and their ability to design and deliver supports to ensure that students with and without disabilities are educated together.

Students with disabilities are seen as belonging primarily to special education teachers. Students without disabilities are seen as general education students.

Students with disabilities and those at risk are explicitly or implicitly tracked and must earn their way out of the lowest track.

Students' struggles are seen as a problem with the individual rather than a problem with instruction.

Only students with IEPs receive accommodations and modifications.

Students with disabilities receive homework help or alternative assignments in segregated settings for part of the day.

THE SOLUTIONS

Build the belief among school teams that every student has value as an individual and is worthy of time, attention, and membership in every opportunity schools and society have to offer.

See students with disabilities as general education students. Provide all students access to specialist-designed strategies. Ensure all students belong to all faculty.

Do not assign any student to a "track"; deliver instruction to students with disabilities in the general education classroom.

Ensure every student receives quality core instruction every day. When students don't respond to instruction, consider changes to the instruction itself.

Provide every student with access to accommodations and modifications when these are needed.

Supply students who need support with evidence-based interventions that support the skill and help them achieve meaningful growth.

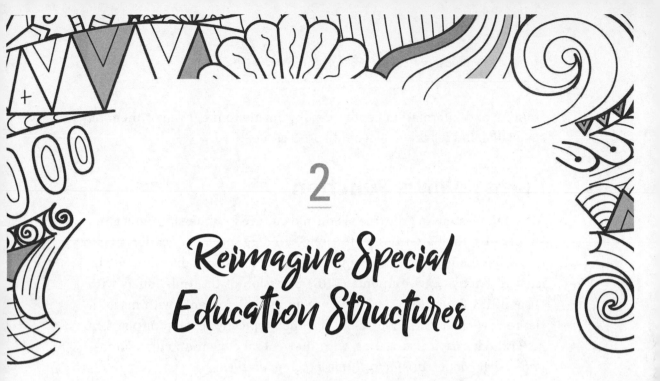

2

Reimagine Special Education Structures

When Kathryn and her son, Jamie, moved to a new school district, she paid a visit to the neighborhood school to enroll him. As Kathryn approached the front desk, the office receptionist smiled and greeted her. But the woman's smile faded when her focus shifted to Jamie, whose disability manifests in physical form. "Oh," the clerk said, pausing for a moment before continuing. "The district has a cluster program for kids like your son. We don't serve them here." She named another elementary school a few miles away and offered to give Kathryn directions.

Kathryn was bewildered. "I didn't even know what a *cluster program* was," she said when relaying the experience to Nancy. "Previously, Jamie had gone to school with all the other neighborhood kids, so this was unexpected and just devastating. I thought, *How is he going to make friends with the neighborhood kids if he doesn't go to school with them?*"

To make a long story short, today Jamie is in his neighborhood school. But Kathryn had to fight to get him there, which meant dealing with the bureaucracy of a district that did not have the capacity to serve him properly. "I've had meetings with district program managers, IEP meetings with teachers and people I never met before," Kathryn said. "The parent training and information center was invaluable to me; I've got them on speed dial. But it has been an uphill process. I'm tired."

Form Follows Function

After taking steps to grow the vision and culture for inclusion, educators should turn their attention to the long-standing special education structures that guide services and supports for students with disabilities. The least restrictive environments (LRE) provision of the Individuals with Disabilities Education Act (IDEA) requires that students with disabilities receive their instruction alongside their typically developing peers, in general education classrooms, with the general education curriculum—*unless they cannot satisfactorily meet their goals there.*

Too often, however, a reverse decision-making process is used. Rather than first trying to meet a student's goals in earnest within the general education curriculum, the IEP team decides on a more restrictive setting and justifies this setting in the IEP they create. In some cases, placement decisions are made primarily according to a student's disability label. But, as we noted in Chapter 1, a disability label actually reveals little about the individual child's specific needs; disability labels should be used to obtain supports and services for students, not to determine these students' educational trajectory.

Although the authors of IDEA were forward-thinking in their day, it's time for us to aim higher. Both the decades-old processes used to determine LRE for students and the resulting service delivery models are ripe for overhaul. But dismantling segregated classes so that students with IEPs can access general education classes more fully is the kind of change that does not happen overnight. It begins with making the decision to do so. Although a transition to inclusive schooling is complex and requires the provision of adequate supporting resource, it must be treated with urgency. Our schools can never be equitable so long as there are still classrooms where only students with disabilities are served.

Systems Capacity and Equitable Education

Disparity in special education placement has been studied for decades. During the 1989–1990 school year, only 3.6 percent of children with intellectual disability in California were placed in general education classrooms, compared to 59.5 percent in Massachusetts (Fisher, Sax, & Pumpian, 1996). Think about that: a child with Down syndrome in the 1980s in Arlington, Massachusetts, was *16 times* more likely to be in a general education class than another child born that same year in Arlington, California. Twenty-five years later, disparities persist. Large urban centers such as New York City, Los Angeles, and Chicago have the most restrictive placements in the country (Brock & Schaefer, 2015). The data are especially discouraging for students with significant disabilities. Although students with high-incidence disabilities (e.g., learning disabilities, health impairments, emotional and behavioral disorders) generally spend 80 percent or more of their day in general education settings, those with low-incidence disabilities (e.g., intellectual disability, multiple disabilities, deafblindness) do not, and this trend has remained stubbornly unchanged since 2001 (Morningstar, Kurth, & Johnson, 2017).

Remember the film *Field of Dreams* (Gordon, Gordon, & Robinson, 1989)? An Iowa farmer was compelled to build a baseball field amid his corn crop, and the act conjured the spirits of a baseball team from long ago. "If you build it, they will come," a voice in the corn told him. And in movie-magic fashion, they did. But this phrase takes on a darker meaning when it comes to segregated settings for students with IEPs. Many districts around the country maintain separate facilities for students with IEPs, generally designated for students who have significant support needs. And, just as predictably, these are filled year after year. Maintaining facilities is a district's fiscal responsibility, and without enrolled students those schools would need to be closed, right? But do students belong in those settings? And are those students receiving the free, appropriate public education (FAPE) they have a right to?

The practice Kathryn encountered—being directed to a separate facility that the district maintained for students with her son's disability diagnosis—clearly violates placement considerations as delineated in federal law. According to a letter to the states from the U.S. Department of Education on IDEA, schools specifically *may not* make a placement decision based on any of the following factors:

- The category of disability
- The configuration of the delivery system
- The availability of educational or related services
- Availability of space
- Administrative convenience

Kathryn learned firsthand that a child's disability label does not predict where that child will be served. Often, it's geography that matters more, which is to say, the school system's capacity to provide supports and services at particular locations predicts placement. Proof of this can be found in the examination of varying placement rates across districts in relation to disability type. Morrier and Gallagher (2010) analyzed the special education placements of 69,000 preschool children in five southern U.S. states. Among their findings was that children in Tennessee were educated in inclusive settings at rates that were higher than children in North Carolina. These two states share a border of a few hundred miles. Do young children with disabilities in Tennessee differ from those in North Carolina to a degree that educating them in an inclusive setting is less of an option? The more likely explanation is that the states' capacity or willingness to provide such opportunities differs. The result is that young children with the same or similar needs and diagnoses living mere miles apart have a completely different educational experience—and, likely, diverging outcomes.

Differences in service delivery begin even before preschool. In studies of early intervention services for children from birth to age 3, disparities in services are already evident (Raspa, Hebbeler, Bailey, & Scarborough, 2010). Lee Ann and her colleague also found that family or community income level predicted whether children aged birth to 3 years received certain services and how much of those individual services were delivered (Jung & Akers, 2016). In particular, they found that families in lower-income neighborhoods whose children qualified for early intervention were less likely to receive speech and physical therapy and received fewer hours of these services. The opposite was true for special instruction; children from higher-income neighborhoods received less special instruction and more specialized therapy services.

Such practices continue. A national analysis of data on the extent to which students with autism participate in general education (Kurth, 2015) revealed a wide variability from state to state. In three states (Montana, New Mexico, and West Virginia), no students with autism were educated in a "separate setting," defined as a separate school, residential school, or home/hospital setting. But in New Jersey, 31 percent of students with autism were educated in separate settings, "further suggesting that there are issues beyond child characteristics that affect educational placements" (p. 254). In places with an extensive network of public and private school settings exclusively for students with IEPs, more restrictive placement practices are rampant (the District of Columbia, Delaware, New York, and Maryland round out the top 5). Conversely, in places where separate facilities are rare (e.g., Oklahoma, Texas), so are such restrictive placements. The individualized instructional opportunities envisioned by IDEA are only made possible by *expanding* access to LRE through response to intervention and multileveled systems of support, and by structured decision making where resources and intervention are based on student needs, not a disability label.

For parents like Kathryn, these aren't just studies and statistics; this is her son. She isn't concerned about the convenience of the adults who run these programs. She sees Jamie as a whole person who needs to make friends, get invited to birthday parties, and accompany other children when they go trick-or-treating on Halloween. All of these typical activities and interactions become so much more difficult when children don't attend their neighborhood school. The bottom line is that the demographics of a family or neighborhood or the characteristics of a service system should not direct placement decisions. Just because there is a building does not mean it must be filled. "If you build it, they will come" is OK for the movies, but not for education.

Institutional factors go beyond facilities and can take the form of working relationships among school personnel. The school psychologist is an influential member of the IEP team, in large part because initial assessment data are used to determine whether students qualify for special education services, and because triennial assessments are administered to determine whether these supports and services are still warranted. Yet pressure to influence placement decisions has been reported repeatedly in the profession. Half of school psychologists reported that they had been instructed by administrators "to avoid recommending support services due to cost . . . and agree with overly restrictive special education placements" (Boccio, Weisz, & Lefkowitz, 2016, p. 669). Perhaps it bears stating: cost containment is not a valid factor in making placement decisions.

Does your school district maintain separate school settings and cluster programs? How many segregated special education classrooms are currently on your school campus? The very existence of these buildings, programs, and segregated classrooms contribute to latent pressure on some administrators. Such tensions can lead to attempts to influence placement decisions and ultimately perpetuate outdated models.

Educators must attend to the programmatic variables that influence education placement not only on behalf of students with disabilities and the people who love and care about them, but also because such decisions reflect larger issues about equity in education. Students with disabilities are not the only students affected by older service structures in need of attention. Similar disparities and regressions exist in the educational experience of students living in poverty, especially those who identify as Latinx or African American, in what has been termed *re-segregation* (Reardon, Grewal, Kalogrides, & Greenberg, 2012). With this re-segregation has come a renewed attention to equity-driven reform. Nationally, schools today are increasingly segregated by race. Between 2001 and 2014, enrollment of Latinx and African American students in resource-poor schools (i.e., those with free/reduced-price lunch rates of 75–100%) increased by 11 percent (U.S. Government Accountability Office [GAO], 2016). Less widely known is that students with disabilities are disproportionately represented in these high-poverty, mostly Latinx- and African American–populated schools (GAO, 2016).

Segregating students with disabilities into institutional and programmatic cul-de-sacs is an indication that the learning environment is not attuned to the needs of the students in it. Harmful placement practices limit the promise of LRE and harm all students in the school. The reverse is also true. Inclusive practices don't just the benefit individual students; they benefit the whole institution. A school, a district, or a state cannot claim to be invested in equity reform for students living in poverty and for other marginalized groups if, at the same time, it fails to interrogate exclusionary practices for students with disabilities.

The Infused Skills Grid: Making Informed Placement Decisions

Lee Ann remembers visiting an occupational therapist's room at a public early primary school. The therapist had pulled three kindergartners from their general education classroom to work on the fine-motor skill of cutting with scissors. They were all seated at a table and had sheets of colored paper, each with several shapes printed on it. The students were cutting out the shapes, and the therapist walked around helping each to adjust the grip on the scissors or hold the paper slightly differently. Lee Ann noticed that the table where the children were sitting looked exactly like the table in the kindergarten classroom she'd been in earlier. Some of the scissors were adapted, but there was no reason these adapted scissors couldn't be used in the regular kindergarten classroom. The lessons plans in the kindergarten classroom offered authentic opportunities to cut with scissors. So why had these three kindergartners been removed from the kindergarten classroom and taken to a segregated room, away from their peers, to work on cutting with scissors? It was simply because their diagnostic testing verified that they had a fine-motor delay and had an IEP goal to master this skill.

Too often, IEP goals are used as a daily scheduler. Nancy recalls a group of students who had significant disabilities and were learning important cause-and-effect concepts in a special education classroom. The elaborate schedule posted on the board, chronicling all the IEP goals of the students and when they would be working toward them, designated 10:00 to 10:30 a.m. as "switch-toy time." Deliberative turning of switches on and off using eye movements would allow these students to operate their motorized wheelchairs and communication devices with increasing degrees of independence—crucial cognitive and motoric skills for these students to learn. But clustering such learning into a 30-minute time period and providing little application opportunity in other environments does not lead to generalization of a skill. These students could be attending their neighborhood schools, where they would get a chance to use switches throughout the day: operating a spin art machine in art class, turning the music on and off in PE, turning on a fan for the teacher, advancing slides during a presentation, or sharing jokes programmed into an assistive communication device with other students. With so many authentic opportunities to apply this skill, they might master the IEP goal in the span of a semester.

Supporting students with significant intellectual and physical disabilities requires thought and planning. An infused skills grid can support IEP teams in making effective placement decisions *and* spawn conversations about service delivery, thus meeting the promise of LRE. In this process, the general education classroom and curriculum are the default, and teams conduct an ecological inventory of the school day to determine where students might be able to work toward their IEP goals.

The infused skills grid provides teams with the structure needed to guide conversations about where supports are delivered and to determine if there is, indeed, a legitimate rationale for removing a student from the general education activity or setting to provide intervention. The infused skills grid is a meshing of the student's priority skills and the settings where the student spends time each day. In secondary schools, these settings are most often the student's class schedule but can also include routines such as morning arrival, lunch, breaks, and so forth. For younger children, elementary school settings include spaces in the classroom (e.g., reading corner, science center), routines of the day (e.g., circle time, center time), and places in the school (e.g., classroom, lunchroom, playground).

High school junior Caroline, whose skill grid is shown in Figure 2.1, is working on developing her written communication skills. In particular, she wants to improve her ability to express complex thoughts in a clear and organized way with rich, sensory language that is easy for the reader to follow and understand. Caroline's grid includes English 11, Chemistry,

Figure 2.1

SAMPLE SECONDARY INFUSED SKILLS GRID: CAROLINE

Setting	Skills		
	Organized, clear, descriptive writing	Confidence in speaking in groups	Conventions of writing
English 11	X	X	X
Chemistry		X	X
Government	X	X	X
Algebra II		X	
Physical Education		X	
Visual Arts		X	

Government, Algebra II, Physical Education, and Visual Arts. Her team discussed in what settings she could work on and get support with improving the clarity and language in her writing skills. English class was an easy first checkmark. But they also agreed that there were many opportunities for her to develop as a writer in both social studies and her art class. The team continued this process for Caroline's goal of developing confidence in oral communication in groups and for her goal of improving in conventions of writing. At the end of the conversation, every skill had a checkmark in a general education setting. This is almost always the case! If there are adequate opportunities to work on and support the skill within the general education settings, there is no justification for removing the student from the general education setting for intervention. Jaquis's grid in Figure 2.2 reveals similar opportunities for meeting intervention needs within his generalized routine.

Figure 2.2
SAMPLE ELEMENTARY INFUSED SKILLS GRID: JAQUIS

Setting	Skills		
	Engaging in challenging work	Impulse control	Reading fluency
Morning arrival/circle		X	
Shared reading	X	X	X
Learning centers	X	X	
Independent reading	X		X
Writing	X	X	
Mathematics		X	
Lunch		X	
Science	X		X
Social Studies	X	X	
Specials (Art, PE, Music)		X	

There will be times when IEP teams identify a skill requiring a support strategy that cannot be implemented in the general education classroom. This sometimes happens with certain speech articulation skills; goals that require private counseling; or for a short-term, Tier 3 intervention. Times in which skills need to be supported outside the general education settings are nuanced, are not common, and should never be seen as a reason to sentence a student to a year of segregated services for a predetermined amount of the day. Whenever support or intervention is needed outside the general education settings, teams should regard this arrangement as temporary and, again, based on skills. This means that students with and without disabilities who need support with the skill are included in the arrangement. IEP teams should revisit the grid and hold conversations about supports and settings on a regular basis, asking questions such as whether the student is having success with these supports, if a change is needed to the supports, and whether supports are still needed at all.

Inclusive Service Delivery

Conversations about LRE need to be accompanied by conversations about least restrictive *service delivery*. Although the most restrictive service delivery occurs outside the general education classroom, there is still a continuum of service delivery *inside* the general education classroom. The evolving vision of inclusive education means choosing both the LRE *and* the least restrictive service delivery model.

Three questions can help identify whether your school's service delivery model is truly inclusive:

1. Is the service helping the student to access the general curriculum?
2. Could the strategies have been delivered within the context of the lessons or activities all students were participating in?
3. Was it necessary for a specialist to implement the strategy, or could it have been delivered by a peer or other adult?

Explore Role Release

One argument for maintaining segregated facilities, programs, and classrooms for students with disabilities is that the setup is conducive to providing more intervention—a higher dosage, as it were. Following this line of logic, students who are two or three grade levels below their peers could not get the support they need in a general education classroom. Given that they have prerequisite goals they need to achieve, doesn't it just make sense to deliver intervention in a special education classroom, where the experts in special education can provide them with what they need for many hours (or all day) each day? The argument is that a student with an IEP couldn't possibly receive the same amount of intervention in a general education classroom in which the content is out of reach.

Giving LRE the reform attention it needs means thinking beyond placement and looking instead to service delivery models. Although an inclusive setting is a necessary condition for inclusive service delivery, on its own, it's not enough. It's possible to meet the letter of the law by having a student spend the full day in a general education classroom and yet still miss the mark on meeting that student's needs. In short, the location of service delivery is only one component of an inclusive service delivery model.

Moving the location of services from segregated settings to integrated ones doesn't guarantee inclusive intervention delivery. After all, there are plenty of examples of exclusion in general education classrooms. Some schools cluster a number of students with disabilities into a handful of general education classrooms, straining teachers' ability to meet these students' needs. Other schools provide special education services within the general education classroom but in a segregated manner. For example, a speech-language pathologist may go into a general education classroom, direct a student to a desk in the corner, and work directly with that student as if in a clinic. A one-on-one paraprofessional may be in a general education classroom to support a single student's activities throughout the day, which can create a harmful level of dependence. Although these services are delivered in the general education classroom, technically obeying the letter of the law by educating students with disabilities in the least restrictive environment, this type of service delivery is clearly not in the spirit of the Individuals with Disabilities Education Act.

In order to answer questions about the dosage of intervention individual students may need, we first need to understand the difference between an *intervention* and a *service*. Consider an adult who needs physical therapy services. You've probably been in this situation or at least known someone who has. Physical therapists move your affected body part into a variety of positions as they assess the situation. After that, they design the best approach to help you heal or gain functional movement. Almost always the physical therapist concludes the session by assigning homework—a set of movements or exercises to do. The therapist does not say, "Great job! Now you go home and rest and don't worry about a thing. I'll handle all the therapy next time you're here. See you next week." Nope. The therapist stresses how important it is for you to follow through with the prescribed plan of exercise, probably many times each day. Why? Because the plan won't work otherwise. One therapy session a week or even a couple of times a week isn't going to cut it. The *intervention*—in this case, the prescribed exercises—needs to be delivered many times a day, because more intervention is better. But just because more intervention is better doesn't mean you need to visit the physical therapist for their *services* several times a day. You are perfectly capable of carrying out the *intervention* that the therapist designed on your own and away from the therapist's office.

Lee Ann's first job as a special education teacher in the mid-1990s was in a segregated school in rural Alabama. Every child in her classroom had a developmental delay or disability, and several received physical therapy services. A physical therapist was only available to the school once a month, however, so the therapist trained other adults at the school to deliver the interventions she designed so that students could receive intervention many times each day. Our point is that when specialists aren't available to implement the intervention, other people can. This is not to say that everyone on the team can design or prescribe every type of intervention. Certainly, if a student needs physical therapy strategies, the physical therapist is the only one qualified to determine what those strategies are and how they should be used. But designing the strategies and *implementing* them can be two different roles.

Some school personnel believe that specialists are the only ones qualified to implement the intervention they design. But does the adult who is receiving physical therapy need to have a degree in physical therapy in order to follow through with recommendations? Of course not. Board-certified behavior analysts (BCBAs) may have advanced training and experience in analyzing complex behaviors and designing intervention plans to support behavior change. But these people do not have magic wands; they have information. Anything they implement, they can teach another person on the team to do. BCBAs may conduct assessments, make recommendations, and even recommend a certain number of hours of intervention. But BCBAs can provide such support as a consultant; the intervention may then be implemented in inclusive settings with adults and peers who are already in that environment. A classroom teacher, parent, or peer, when trained, can effectively implement strategies to improve a variety of areas of development or behavior.

This idea of *role release*, or consultative services delivery, has its roots in the field of medicine. Decades ago, when children needed to have gastrostomy tubes for feeding or tracheotomies for breathing, they were usually institutionalized. Only a physician or nurse could care for a person with such intensive health care needs. But sometime in the 1990s, hospitals began training families to provide this medical care for their children. Sure, it took the expertise of the medical team to show families how to feed their children with G-tubes and how to suction tracheotomies, but the families learned. The doctors and nurses didn't have magic wands; they had information. Families with all kinds of backgrounds learned these medical procedures, they took their children home, and their children lived. Not only do we need to presume competence in the students we serve, but we also need to have faith in our team members.

Role release also upends, in many ways, the status quo of frequency and intensity of services. Rather than accessing services (i.e., calling on a specialist) based on how often students need intervention, the service is provided based on the intensity and frequency that the *adults* need. In this new conceptualization of LRE, severity of the student's disability does not direct service decisions in inclusive setting; rather, "How much support does the adult need?" is the guiding question.

Casey is a second-year teacher at a small, rural elementary school. This year, one of her students, Connor, has a diagnosis of autism. Connor's IEP team developed a goal that he will use a picture communication schedule to help him transition between activities and places. How often does Connor need services to support his goal of successfully using a picture communication schedule? Casey has never worked with a student with autism and has never used a picture communication schedule. Because she needs more support, more service will be needed for a while—but only until Casey has mastered providing the kind of support that Connor needs.

Janis is another teacher at the school. She has 15 years of teaching experience, and over the years, she has used picture communication schedules with eight other children. She has also modified and designed picture communication schedules. In Janis's class, Connor would need less of the *service* in order to get the same amount of *intervention*.

Similarly, a "dump and hope" approach of simply placing students with IEPs in general education classrooms without sophisticated systems to support them is not acceptable. This is harmful to students—and to the general and special educators who have dedicated their professional lives to positively affecting the learning of their students. But we can't use the lack of resources as justification for telling a family we are unable to meet their needs—the only action the lack of resources justifies is putting resources into place.

Share Responsibilities and Resources

When schools and districts place too many students with disabilities into too few classrooms, they stretch the capacity of both general and special educators and prevent them from teaching effectively. We have personally witnessed the deleterious effects of this practice. Over the years, in different schools, we have been asked for advice about how to improve student achievement, school climate, and so on. Our first whiff of the source of the problem occurs when we are escorted to a designated "inclusion classroom" (which implies there also exist "exclusion classrooms").

There are several reasons why this approach—having only certain classrooms responsible for teaching a wide range of students together—fails to create equitable and inclusive schools. Some argue that this is an efficient use of resources, but as we will see in the paragraphs that follow, there are simply too many compromises to believe that it is an effective way of organizing resources and supports. For one, it violates the natural proportions of the population. If students with disabilities make up 10 percent of a school's population, then a similar percentage of these students should be present in all the classes as resources and responsibilities become shared. In addition, when natural proportions are followed, disability is normalized and naturalized—not concentrated. When only some classes have the opportunity to educate students with and without disabilities together, the proportion of students with disabilities within some classes can double. A district Nancy once worked for had a name for it: the *supersaturation model*, in which students with disabilities make up 33 percent of a class overseen by a full-time special educator and a full-time general educator. There are even schools and districts that raise the percentage of students with disabilities in some classes to 50 percent. As a special educator who operated within this model, Nancy can confirm it didn't work.

If you ask Julie, a school-based special education coordinator, she will say this model doesn't work because it succeeds only in magnifying the perception of the disability, a phenomenon that occurs when you observe people with similar characteristics in close proximity to one another. Attending a family reunion, for example, you might suddenly be struck by how many of your relatives resemble one another. Everywhere you look, you see the same eyes or the same chin. A similar thing can happen in the supersaturation model classroom: the common manifestation of a disability obscures the individuals' unique traits and abilities. The logic behind this organization is that it allows for resources to be concentrated. The reality is that there aren't sufficient peer supports and peer models, and expectations can become skewed.

If you ask Doug, the supersaturation model doesn't work because it taxes the personnel in the school. Usually those enlisted to teach classes with very high percentages of students with disabilities are general education teachers who have been deemed highly skilled and special educators with excellent collaboration skills. In some ways, it's a performance punishment that disincentivizes educators to improve their practice. While the skilled teachers are tapped for this extra-challenging work, other teachers remain static. They aren't asked to create equitable learning conditions, and they aren't asked to de-privatize their practice to collaborate with others. The selective use of personnel also tends to foster feelings of unfairness and even resentment; teachers wonder, "Why does my job have to be harder because someone else isn't doing their job?" Over time, this can contribute to burnout in both general and special educators (Embich, 2001).

Nancy will say that clustering a large number of students with support needs in a single classroom makes developing and implementing meaningful accommodations and modifications much more difficult. Meeting with small groups of students for pre-teaching and re-teaching is more complicated when a significant portion of the class needs such support. In Nancy's experience, supersaturation classrooms rely more on whole-group instruction, supplanting time that otherwise could be dedicated to more precise supports. Although access to the general curriculum is often incorrectly assumed to be solely a function of location, a student's access to the curriculum is also affected by the instructional arrangement and curricular adaptations within the general education classroom. When students with disabilities receive more flexible, small-group instruction rather than whole-group, their access to general curriculum increases—and this is true as well when they receive curricular adaptations (Soukup, Wehmeyer, Bashinski, & Bovaird, 2007).

Solving a problem begins by recognizing that one exists. You can determine whether your school has an equitable distribution of students throughout classes by comparing the percentage of students with disabilities in your school or district to the percentage within general education classes. Classes with percentages that are substantially higher or lower than the natural proportion warrant closer inspection. Whether this is due to institutional habit or the other factors we've outlined, such analysis is important to the process of establishing a truly inclusive service delivery model. Ensuring an equitable composition across classrooms is the first step toward achieving the goal of creating conditions that increase and support the effectiveness of educators.

Use Paraprofessional Support Effectively

The use of paraprofessionals has increased in schools more than any other service in the past 30 years (Wagner, Newman, Cameto, Levine, & Marder, 2003), and these individuals provide valuable support for students. However, the practice of many schools is to assign paraprofessionals to provide one-on-one support to students with more significant needs throughout the day. Special education paraprofessionals cost less than certificated teachers, and for these schools, the thinking is that (1) having another adult in the room will lessen the demand on the general education teacher, and (2) the student otherwise would not be able to participate or access the curriculum. But this is a blunt tool for creating supports, takes attention away from the curricular and technology supports that should also be deployed, and can thwart student independence (Giangreco, 2010). Reflecting on the questions we introduced at the beginning of this chapter, the focus should be on whether assigning this adult to help this student throughout the day increases access to the curriculum and enhances the student's participation.

Consider, for example, Pierre, an 8th grade student with autism. His parents recently relocated and enrolled him in the local middle school. Pierre uses some verbal language to communicate, but he communicates primarily through assistive technology. He had been enrolled in general education classes at his previous school, but the special education coordinator at his new school said this would be possible only if he had a paraprofessional with him all day. Pierre's parents recognized that he needed some extra support, but they worried that with an adult following him everywhere, every day, it would be difficult for him to make friends—which was already a challenge. Is this truly inclusion?

Even though the intent of providing a paraprofessional for a specific student is well meaning, and often seen by schools as necessary for students with physical, behavioral, or intellectual disabilities, implementation often leads to more harm than good. Assigning a paraprofessional to a student can disrupt that child's relationships with friends and teachers, impede learning opportunities, and create dependencies (Giangreco, 2010).

To the other students in the class, the presence of the paraprofessional signals that this student is different. The social dynamics of school are challenging enough, and it's already difficult for many students to navigate them and develop friendships; the ever-present paraprofessional presents yet another barrier. In classrooms where a paraprofessional is assigned to a student, interactions with classmates are limited (see Carter, Sisco, Brown, & Brickham, 2008). The majority of the student's interactions are with the paraprofessional. Students with significant disabilities rarely get an opportunity to learn alongside their classmates, as the paraprofessional becomes the student's default learning partner (Feldman, Carter, Asmus, & Brock, 2016).

Having an adult attached to a child all day, every day, is also a signal of low expectations. It's an arrangement that says, "We don't expect this student will ever be more independent than he is now" or "We expect that this student is the one in the classroom who will always need the most support." These messages are neither inclusive nor accurate.

Further, this practice impedes opportunities for students to learn academic content as well as social skills. From the general education teacher's perspective, the student is already being supported by someone and receiving individual attention and feedback. Because of this, general education teachers are less likely to support a student who is assigned a paraprofessional in the natural way they support every other child in the classroom (Giangreco, Yuan, McKenzie, Cameron, & Fialka, 2005). So the student with a paraprofessional is isolated both from friends and from the general education teacher.

Exclusive reliance on individual personal supports is also not the best way to position students for future success. It can be difficult to find paid one-to-one support after the school years. There is no special education McDonald's or Nordstrom. People with disabilities are either included in the community or they are not. On the job, they rely on the natural supports of the work environment. Residential support is not one-to-one unless it's from a roommate.

Evidence spanning more than a decade warns about the risk of detrimental social and academic outcomes resulting from using paraprofessionals as one-on-one aides for students with disabilities. This type of support should be seen on the least restrictive service continuum as the most restrictive option within a general education classroom—an example of "excluding practices in an inclusive setting." Assigning a one-on-one paraprofessional should be a last resort and a temporary solution, rather than a default for any student included in the general education classroom (Giangreco, 2010). Any time you can select natural supports rather than specialized ones, you have made a more inclusive choice.

Sometimes classrooms need more than one adult to run smoothly and ensure everyone succeeds. How can schools use paraprofessional support in a way that leads to positive outcomes for students? To use a basketball analogy, what's required is a zone defense, not man-to-man coverage. The paraprofessional in the inclusive general education classroom provides occasional one-on-one support to the student with disabilities who needs it while also interacting and supporting other students, including students without disabilities.

The paraprofessional in an inclusive classroom is a crucial bridge between general and special educators, but to make the most of this team-based model, grade-level or department teams should think strategically when planning lessons and routines about where support would be most useful. When paraprofessionals are provided to the group rather than assigned to a specific student, the extra adult is less likely to limit social opportunities for students (Hillesøy, 2016). In this way, as discussed in Chapter 1, need (rather than disability status) guides the instructional decisions.

Carlos has cerebral palsy and often needs physical support throughout the day. His parents also want him to be independent and make friends. At a meeting, the 2nd grade team discussed how to support him given his class's daily schedule and routines. In Carlos's class, during morning "centers" time, some children worked in the writing center, others in the computer center, and yet others in independent work areas. His teacher mentioned that there was often a lot of chaos in the computer center; many children needed support in navigating the new math software and just generally using and taking care of the computers. The team decided that, during morning centers time, the paraprofessional should be mostly in the computer area to support any student who needed it. The general education teacher planned to take the lead in the writing center, because students frequently made requests for feedback and help in this center. In this way, the team acknowledged Carlos's likely needs and prepared to support him—and any other student. This arrangement is also flexible enough to allow the teacher and paraprofessional to step into another zone to meet Carlos's needs or the needs of any other student. This use of paraprofessional support helps Carlos when he requires help, but it also allows him to take on new tasks so he can grow, learn, and interact with his peers.

Special education paraprofessionals are members of a school's instructional team. In this model of inclusion, they provide intermittent support to students with IEPs and assist the general education teacher in ways that benefit all of the students in the class, including supervising collaborative groups of students and facilitating peer supports (see Figure 2.3).

Enlist the Natural Support of Peers

Moving away from the overuse of one-on-one paraprofessionals is an important step toward allowing natural classroom resources to

Figure 2.3
SUPPORT STRUCTURES FOR PARAPROFESSIONALS

If the teacher is . . .	The paraprofessional can . . .
Taking attendance	Collect and review homework
Giving directions	Write the directions on the board, providing visual cues for all students
Providing large-group instruction	Model note taking on the board; implement curricular accommodations or modifications as needed
Giving a test	Assist individuals or small groups who require assistance
Facilitating stations or small groups	Support students within stations or small groups, at the teacher's direction
Facilitating silent reading	Assist students with reading material selection; redirect as needed
Teaching a new concept	Present visuals or models to enhance student understanding
Re-teaching or pre-teaching with a small group	Monitor the larger group of students

blossom—and there's no support that's more natural than a student's classmates. Studies spanning decades show that peer-to-peer supports yield powerful academic and social benefits for students with disabilities (e.g., Dunn, Shelnut, Ryan, & Katsiyannis, 2017; Okilwa & Shelby, 2010). One of the reasons peer support is so effective is the increased opportunity students have to respond to and gain feedback from others (Hattie & Timperley, 2007). High school students with IEPs who are in segregated classrooms have smaller social networks and "fewer opportunities to draw on support compared with students in more inclusive settings" (Fisher & Shogren, 2016, p. 96).

Students who serve in the mentor role also benefit from the arrangement, and this is not limited to students who are high-achieving; even when the mentor students are struggling with the content, the positive outcomes are still achieved. The mentor and mentee each make academic and social gains (Cushing & Kennedy, 1997). And here is good news for inclusive classrooms: general education teachers report that, with proper training, they find it easy to implement peer-to-peer support strategies within their classroom routines (Bowman-Perrott et al., 2013).

Many educators have seen how peer supports benefit students with disabilities. The advance of special education research means they now have data to back up their anecdotal evidence. Peer support arrangements meet the Council for Exceptional Children's standards for evidence-based instruction, as reported in Brock and Huber's 2017 systematic review of related studies. Examples of social and academic peer supports include the following (Carter, Moss, Hoffman, Chung, & Sisko, 2011):

- Greeting one another
- Socializing before class begins
- Introducing the student with a disability to other peers
- Encouragement during tasks
- Discussing assignments
- Brainstorming ideas at the beginning of an assignment
- Scribing a written task for the student with a disability

Most of these supports sound much like the ones teachers furnish for all students in a classroom. For students with more significant disabilities, supports might be intentionally delivered by peers who have received explicit training in how to do so. As we describe in Chapter 3, one role for special educators is to oversee peer support training, including meeting with students to engage in problem solving as challenges arise.

Conclusion

Qualifying for an IEP is not justification for receiving services in a segregated setting. The LRE provision of IDEA requires that students be moved to more restrictive settings *only if they cannot accomplish their IEP goals within the general education setting*. Often, though, focused conversation around where services and supports are to be delivered is nonexistent. Over and over again, we have seen teams make the decision to put "resource room" onto a student's high school schedule with the purpose of helping the student to stay afloat with assignments. For these students, disability status is used as the justification for reserving a generic, catch-all space in the day for pullout services. This is a convenient arrangement for the school, but it misses the entire point of special education services. The mission is not to drag kids through assignments; it is to change their lives—give them a solid foundation of skills that will maximize their success in school and beyond. Students are cheated out of this opportunity when special educators are shunted into the role of playing proverbial whack-a-mole as homework helpers—a waste of their expertise. To ensure that there is purposeful attention to teaching students skills (and to be in compliance with the LRE provisions of IDEA), conversations must shift away from disability categories and assignments to skills, the type of support that is needed to develop those skills, and the natural settings where that support can be delivered.

Building bridges between special and general educators results in collaboration, the sharing of expertise, and ultimately improved teaching and student outcomes. Rather than duplicating efforts and operating in silos, inclusive schools and districts can create new ways to work together. If the mission of a school is to help all students belong and succeed, rather than to create the most convenient structure for the adults, then the moral imperative is clear.

Changing Placement and Service Delivery Models

THE CHALLENGES

Existing institutional factors direct placement of students with disabilities into separate schools, disability-specific cluster programs, and designated special education or resource classrooms.

The capacity of a system predicts student participation in general education. If a school does not have sufficient capacity, students with IEPs spend less time in general education classes.

Service frequency and intensity are determined based on the severity of the student's disability. More severe disability categories warrant more frequent and intense services.

Supports do not vary. The same amount of support is provided across the year, across learning environments, and across assignment types.

The amount of service a student gets remains the same from year to year, because it is based on norms for the school or the student's diagnosis.

THE SOLUTIONS

Determine placement after outcomes are set and by asking whether any time in a more restrictive environment is necessary to achieve each outcome.

Individualize each placement decision based on needs, not diagnosis. This produces natural variation in service frequency and intensity.

Determine the frequency and intensity of service based on how much support the adults in the general education setting require in order to deliver effective interventions and ensure success on outcomes.

Use an infused skills grid in IEP team settings to carefully consider the extent to which any student with a disability needs to be removed from the general education classroom. Have teams examine the general curriculum for opportunities to deliver interventions and teach targeted skills.

Vary the amount of support each student and the general education teachers receive—from year to year and within the year—based on the current needs of the student. Do not allow any student to spend all year "in the resource room" just because there is a place in the schedule for this assignment.

3

Leverage the Strengths of All Educators

Newly hired to teach at an elementary school, Nancy sat in a large auditorium, watching the school district's other new teachers find seats. After inspiring speeches by the superintendent and other district leaders, the attendees were invited to scan the day's agenda: a review of employee benefit plans, contract requirements, and logistics. Concurrent orientation sessions would be held for elementary and secondary teachers, and a *separate* orientation would be held for the special education teachers.

Nancy was taken aback; nothing on the agenda was related to education-specific issues. When she inquired why special educators would be separated from the other teachers, an event staffer replied, "We've always done it this way." The school district was sending a clear message that it believed special education and general education to be fundamentally different.

The Great (False) Divide

This division between general and special education, entrenched in many schools, is reinforced on the first day of most teacher preparation programs.

All four of us chose special education as a career only to discover that choosing special education meant turning away from general education. Preservice special education teachers do not share courses with those studying general education, and at many colleges and universities, the curriculum is delivered by separate university departments. This traditional arrangement has serious consequences. Special education is governed by the principle of the least restrictive environment (LRE), but how can special educators support this without understanding what general education is? How can general educators embrace educating students with disabilities when they have had little preparation for and experience with this part of their job?

When Doug was an aspiring speech-language pathologist, he worked as an intern at an elementary school with a large cluster program for children who were Deaf. Doug was providing pullout services for two 5th graders, unaware that their general education science class had been studying plate tectonics, and that afternoon was the big event: a model of a volcano was going to erupt. After their language intervention session, Doug escorted the two back to their classroom just in time to see their peers rejoicing—the volcano had just erupted, but the boys had missed it. One began to cry; the other scowled. Doug realized that he could have easily adapted his lesson to be delivered within the science classroom. In fact, it would have been more authentic to practice communication skills in the context of a hands-on science demonstration. But because Doug had no connection to the general education curriculum, he had no inkling that he should have done so. Those two boys weren't the only ones who were struck by the inherent unfairness of the situation.

Similarly, general educators are often kept at arm's length from professional learning and planning meetings for students with individualized education programs (IEPs). The exception is when they are asked to fulfill the mandate that general education be represented at the annual IEP meeting. More often than not, this is a minimal compliance situation. We've lost track of the number of IEP meetings we have attended in which there was only one general education teacher present, even though the student whose plan was being discussed had six general education teachers in total. We have also seen those lone general education teachers stay in the room only long enough to report on the student's present level of performance in his or her content area; once this box was checked, the general educator was excused for the remainder of the meeting. We can even recall a few instances in which a random general educator was pulled from the hall at the last minute to ensure compliance with the requirement. How can general education teachers be expected to have a vested interest in the progress of their students with disabilities when they themselves are not fully included the process that articulates how to best meet those students' needs? When special educators box out general educators in this way, the message they are sending is clear: *You aren't the experts on student support. You aren't needed.*

The message is received, and the divide persists. Consider that a study of 239 early childhood and elementary teachers found that the majority of them were not familiar with common positive behavioral support strategies for students with challenging behavior, did not know if their schools engaged in functional behavioral assessments, and were unaware if their school tracked mental health issues (Stormont, Reinke, & Herman, 2011). Keep in mind that these teachers weren't being asked about implementation; they were only asked whether they were *aware*. Clearly, they did not see these evidence-based and best practices as part of the educational fabric of their schools.

Response to intervention (RTI) is a common three-tiered system for supporting the academic achievement of students not yet making expected progress. Yet a 2014 survey of general education teachers found that only 19 percent were able to provide a minimal definition of RTI (three-tiered system, needs-based, and a description of the tiers), even though this process has appeared in law since 2004 (Castro-Villarreal, Rodriguez, & Moore, 2014). Little wonder that these same teachers reported that the RTI process was "overwhelming" and "too long," and cited lack of training as the most significant barrier to implementation (p. 108). If evidence-based interventions are not being provided, more and more students are going to be referred for special education services even though they might simply be undertaught.

Positive behavioral supports and RTI have a special education research base that has informed general education best practices, and both have been further defined through multi-tiered systems of support (MTSS). All have been used to improve the learning lives of students with and without disabilities. But to be effective, such practices rely on cohesive schoolwide structures that involve both general and special education teachers. In other words, they don't work without the full faculty's understanding and schoolwide implementation. In schools where the full faculty is not involved in learning and implementing these initiatives, the success of the practices is low (Burns et al., 2013).

The axiom that the general educator knows content and the special educator knows intervention is outdated and must be changed. In order for inclusive education to thrive, this territorialism must be eliminated. The balkanization of schools and districts has divided caring educators into camps, benefiting neither students nor adults. Essentially, the current status quo in many schools undermines sharing of the rich reserves of varied knowledge that teams possess.

Needless problems are created when outdated organizational systems prevent general and special educators from collaborating. To realize the promise and success of truly equitable and inclusive education, the roles of school leaders, general educators, special educators, and paraprofessionals need to be redefined and reimagined. This in turn requires systems-level changes that support and amplify instruction and intervention efforts.

Redefining Educator Roles

School change requires the efforts of the collective whole, be it to close racial achievement gaps (Gorey, 2009), reduce disciplinary inequities

(Gage, Whitford, & Katsiyannis, 2018), or to support students living in poverty (Wong & Meyer, 1998). The processes of the past that isolate students—and isolate teachers from one another—do not work for teachers and administrators seeking to meet the needs of every student. Because equitable schooling practices, of which inclusive education is a crucial facet, must be schoolwide and not relegated to a few classrooms, it is imperative for teachers have access to one another in ways that transcend licensure. They need chances to collaborate, consult, and engage in professional learning together in meaningful ways.

MTSS and RTI are examples of whole-school practices employed to support students who are not yet making expected progress behaviorally or academically. Both MTSS and RTI intentionally blur the line between general and special education and leverage the collective wisdom of the school. However, any MTSS and RTI initiative is doomed to fail if only the special educators or the newly hired "RTI staff" are asked to do this work. The reason is simple: these practices are intended to support students with and without IEPs throughout the school. Schoolwide efforts require schoolwide participation.

Efforts to move to more innovative school staffing structures that support schoolwide initiatives are not without growing pains. In evolving schools, it's common for mistaken assumptions to arise regarding the roles and responsibilities of each member of the team, and these assumptions can lead to gaps in school and district procedures and services to students. Practitioners may find themselves being asked to provide services to a new group of students. Who should complete the report card? Which team member is supposed to schedule parent conferences? Which department is responsible for monitoring course completion requirements so that students can move on to high school? Such oversights can lead to misunderstandings, subpar services, and even legal action.

This redefinition of roles and responsibilities does not require any redistribution of funds. Rather, these are shared agreements about the roles of the special educator, general educator, and paraprofessional at the intersection of five major shared responsibilities: instruction, assessment, communication, leadership, and record keeping. Figure 3.1 provides an overview of each of these responsibilities.

The Role of the Special Educator

Historically, special educators have been trained in categorical programs that emphasize instructional approaches based on or geared toward particular disabilities and focus little on general pedagogy. Further, special educators have been expected to provide intervention within more restrictive settings, such as a resource room or a self-contained classroom. Until recent years, few special education teacher preparation programs offered experiences within the general education curriculum.

Today, more special educators are being prepared to provide their services in inclusive classrooms and schools. The practitioners in the field, who are continuing to redefine their roles in these inclusive environments, are discovering that their responsibilities are shifting to more collaborative arrangements.

Instruction. Special educators provide individual and small-group instruction as they always have, but now they do so in inclusive classrooms. A special educator may be assigned to a general education classroom to re-teach key concepts to a group of students (with and without IEPs). Some may co-teach a class with the content-area teacher, therefore instructing the whole class. Students with IEPs in general education also may require accommodations and modifications of assignments and assessments. Special educators bring ideas for strategies that have been traditionally used in "intervention time" into the classroom to be delivered to all students. These universal design strategies can be implemented at first by the special educator, with the idea that they can be delivered in the future by the general education teacher. Designing each of these components is the rightful responsibility of the special educator; however, carrying out the accommodations and modifications is the responsibility of everyone on the team. Rather than being the sole deliverer of

Figure 3.1

REDEFINING ROLES IN THE INCLUSIVE SCHOOL

Role	Special Educator	General Educator	Paraprofessional
Instruction	• Provides instruction to individual students, small groups, and whole class • Designs accommodations for and modifications of materials and instruction • Monitors students' academic work • Coordinates support for individual students (e.g., medical and behavioral needs)	• Provides instruction to individual students, small groups, and whole class • Differentiates and adjusts instruction to meet student needs • Implements accommodations, modifications, and specially designed instructional strategies	• Follows instructional plans as implemented by the general education teacher • Implements accommodations, modifications, and specialized strategies as designed by the special education teacher • Provides specialized assistance to assigned students as needed (e.g., personal care)
Assessment	• Grades or assists with grading student performance • Measures student progress toward IEP goals • Administers standardized measures • Adapts classroom assessments	• Conducts formative and summative assessments • Grades students on modified expectations • Administers local and state standardized measures • Measures student progress toward IEP goals within daily routines and activities • Provides timely and useful feedback during formative assessment opportunities	• Assists and supports classroom assessment of student performance • Collaborates with general and special education teachers to report student progress on IEP goals

(continued)

Figure 3.1

REDEFINING ROLES IN THE INCLUSIVE SCHOOL (continued)

Role	Special Educator	General Educator	Paraprofessional
Communication	• Attends planning meetings • Communicates with students and families • Attends problem-solving meetings • Provides information for professional development relating to inclusive practices	• Collaborates with the special educator to differentiate curriculum • Provides feedback to families and other team members on the effectiveness of strategies being used • Attends IEP and planning meetings • Collaborates with and provides information to grade-level/subject-area teams on curriculum and instruction • Attends problem-solving meetings	• Provides feedback to team members on the success of strategies • Assists in communicating with parents and families • Maintains effective and open communication with the school • Honors confidentiality of student information
Leadership	• Trains and supervises paraprofessionals • Coordinates peer tutoring • Facilitates use of related services professionals	• Designs the structure of the class (e.g., curriculum, classroom management, physical design, policies, materials) • Supervises paraprofessionals and peer tutors	• Facilitates social relationships between students • Creates a positive and reinforcing environment for students • Models effective communication for other staff
Record keeping	• Leads development of student IEPs • Maintains documentation of progress toward IEP goals • Maintains records of accommodations, modifications, and specially designed instruction	• Records daily lesson and unit plans, activities, and assignments • Maintains student records of progress and grades on learning targets and standards • Maintains attendance records	• Assists the special education teacher in documenting student progress toward IEP goals • Maintains logs and time sheets

interventions and supports, the special educator serves as the primary coordinator of support to address students' academic, behavioral, and medical needs.

Assessment. Administration of education tests and inventories is an important duty for special educators. The interpretation and application of the results of these instruments may also fall to general education teachers or a school psychologist, depending on the nature of the assessment. But the greater change in the assessment role of special educators comes in how they support day-to-day monitoring of students' progress toward achieving classroom learning targets, standards, and individualized goals. It is the special educator's job to lead the team in identifying when a student needs accommodation or modification on classroom assessments and designing how those assessments should look. In the classroom, some special educators collaborate with the general educator in grading students' performance on assignments and teacher-designed tests.

Special educators are also responsible for leading the progress monitoring of students' IEP goal attainment. This is a key duty and one that many schools and states have struggled to fulfill; historically, the area of lowest IDEA compliance for states has been in progress monitoring and reporting (Etscheidt, 2006). It is the special educator's job to outline the specific measures to be used for IEP goals, coordinate data collection, and communicate this progress to students, families, and other team members (Jung, 2018a).

Communication. The special educator in an inclusive school facilitates communication among families, staff, and administrators. Curricular, technological, and personal supports for students with IEPs depend on the timely and accurate exchange of information. Special educators also are charged with communicating progress on IEP goals across the team. These communications occur in planning and problem-solving meetings as well as through conversations and written communication with families. Because special educators also provide information about inclusive practices to staff and administrators, many find it helpful to establish dedicated communication tools, such as an assistance request form to be used by the general education team. They also use student profiles, the infused skills grid, and goal attainment and growth plans (see Chapters 1 and 2) to share information.

Leadership. Supervision and training of paraprofessionals who provide personal supports (now extending throughout the school community) remain the responsibility of the special educator. Some special educators coordinate peer tutoring, including teaching elective classes in which students learn how to provide assistance to other students. They encourage the development of natural supports and friendships by observing peer interactions, modeling support strategies, and then fading prompts to allow the natural supports to emerge. Finally, special educators demonstrate leadership when they collaborate with related services providers (e.g., speech-language pathologists, physical therapists) to identify opportunities to provide services or embed specialized strategies.

Record keeping. To be sure, there is a long tradition of extensive paperwork in special education. The special educator leads the development and scheduling of the IEP meeting and ensures that all team members receive a copy of the document and understand it. The infused skills grid and student profile can assist in this endeavor. As noted, they also lead the effort to measure progress toward IEP goals and maintain records of this progress. To ensure accurate grading and class credits, special educators keep records of accommodations and modifications provided to students.

Technology has allowed the special educator to complete their record-keeping tasks more efficiently. Online communication tools and lesson plans developed in shared online documents ensure everyone has access to real-time updates. Templates of forms can also be developed as online documents or housed on the school's server to make these tools available throughout the school. Online learning management systems and platforms for measuring progress bring efficiency to the process. Digital calendars also allow them to make up-to-the-minute changes in schedules and paraprofessional assignments.

The Role of the General Educator

Like special educators, general education teachers' responsibilities are evolving with the times. In inclusive schools, they teach and endeavor to meet the various needs of a diverse student population. The distribution of funds and resources throughout these inclusive schools also means that they communicate daily with special education staff—teachers, therapists, paraprofessionals, and other support personnel—with whom they once had limited interactions.

To be effective, these new and expanded education teams need clearly defined roles and responsibilities. Like the special educator, the general educator has instructional, assessment, communication, leadership, and record-keeping duties; however, the ways in which these duties are carried out in inclusive schools differ from schools of the past.

Instruction. The primary instruction of all students remains a central job responsibility of the general educator. In inclusive classrooms, the student population has broadened to include a wide range of abilities. This diversity challenges general education teachers to use their full repertoire of instructional arrangements, including individual and small-group instruction as well as traditional large-group delivery. It also means that they look to the special educator as a consultant to help co-design classroom instruction that can meet the needs of the broadest range of skills learners have. General educators must still monitor students' academic progress, but they must also be prepared to use this information in collaboration with other members of the team to identify and implement necessary adaptations to ensure continued growth.

Assessment. Assessments fall into three categories: classroom, standardized, and performance-based. The general educator is responsible for conducting all of these assessments. Classroom assessments are used to monitor progress and guide instructional decisions (formative assessment) and determine mastery of content (summative assessment). In some instances, assessments and grades may be determined collaboratively with the special educator. When modifications to classroom assessments are needed, it is the responsibility of the general educator to implement the modification and to note that the grade is based on a modified expectation (see Chapter 1). In inclusive schools, teams develop systems for noting when assessments are modified so the meaning of the grade can be clearly communicated (Jung, 2017a).

In addition to administering and interpreting typical classroom assessments, general educators are also responsible for measuring the progress that students with disabilities make toward relevant IEP goals. The design of the measurement is led by the special educator, but the actual measurement happens in general education settings. Gone are the days of pulling students to "probe" and administer "trials" to measure progress. What matters is if students are gaining skills and using them in natural, everyday routines and activities. The general educator is the one best suited to see and record this evidence (Jung, 2018a).

State and district standards-based tests are important for gauging progress for individual students and across systems; the inclusion of students who have IEPs in these assessments is an important feature of federal and state special education laws. The majority of students with IEPs take such tests with accommodations only or with no adaptation at all. The IEP team determines the need for accommodations on standardized tests, which should mirror the accommodations students use for classroom assessments. A very small percentage of students (1% of the special education population) take an alternate, or modified, form of standardized assessments. Eligible students have significant disabilities, including intellectual disability.

In schools and districts where performance-based assessment is used or required, the general educators helps students with disabilities develop projects and portfolios, implementing adaptions that have been designed by the special educator.

Communication. Because sound decision making is dependent on timely and accurate information, the sharing of information is critical within inclusive schools. The general educator is responsible for providing the special education teacher with curriculum, materials, and unit plans in a timely fashion so that necessary accommodations and modifications can be developed. When time is allocated for these activities and procedures are followed consistently, students with IEPs are able to fully participate in the classroom and curriculum.

The general educator also provides feedback to the special educator on the effectiveness of strategies. An accommodation that looks great on paper might be inadequate when used in the classroom. Identifying what works and what does not work refines teaching practices. Families and parents should also be a part of the communication loop, and all professionals who support a student should be able to communicate goals and progress to the child's family.

Leadership. The structure and design of the classroom—including curriculum, materials, physical layout, and classroom management policies—are the responsibility of the general educator. In all of these aspects, the special educator can be a valuable resource for ideas and strategies that will effectively support students with IEPs in the classroom environment.

The general education teacher supervises paraprofessionals and peer tutors assigned to the classroom. When these specialized supports are made available for students with IEPs who require additional assistance, it is essential that they complement the instructional routines of the class. The general educator gives immediate feedback and direction to paraprofessionals and peer supports so that these resources are used wisely.

The leadership duties of the general education teacher often extend to the grade-level or content-area team. Many schools require that all staff participate in regularly scheduled planning meetings to discuss curriculum and instruction. Teachers assume leadership of their grade-level teams and professional learning communities. General education teachers also provide supervision and support for classroom assistants and volunteers.

Record keeping. The general educator is responsible for recording unit and daily lesson plans, activities, and homework, as well as maintaining students' grades and attendance records. Records of how students with IEPs perform in general education routines and activities provide the basis for team discussions on support strategies. These classroom assessment data on general curriculum standards and IEP goals are far more important than standardized assessment information when making practical instruction and support decisions.

The Role of the Paraprofessional

Once rare in school, paraprofessionals have become common in contemporary classrooms. In fact, more than 90 percent of U.S. public schools employ paraprofessionals (Hampden-Thompson, Diehl, & Kinukawa, 2007). Sometimes, parents and educators mistakenly assume that the presence of another adult is all that is needed to sufficiently support a student who has an IEP. Like the other team members, a paraprofessional in an inclusive school needs clearly defined roles and responsibilities in order for these supports to work. Like other members of the education team, paraprofessionals have duties in the areas of instruction, assessment, communication, leadership, and record keeping.

Instruction. The paraprofessional implements lesson plans as designed by the general education teacher. Paraprofessionals also provide designed accommodations and modifications to any student who needs them, but they are careful to avoid "accidental modifications" in which they provide so much support that it actually changes what students learn.

Although paraprofessionals are not responsible for delivering primary instruction to students, they can re-teach skills to individuals and small groups of students who need additional time and experience with the material. The paraprofessional in the inclusive classroom provides specialized support on an as-needed basis to students with IEPs and general support to the rest of the class as directed by the classroom teacher. It is essential that paraprofessionals are *not* assigned to a single student. In fact, this type of assignment is detrimental to the relationships of students with their teachers and with peers, and fosters dependence. And this is only the beginning of the negative outcomes associated with this model of connecting a "shadow teacher," "one-on-one aide," or "personal assistant" to a single child (Giangreco, 2010). When specialized supports are necessary for a particular student, the paraprofessional follows precise guidelines for their nature, duration, and frequency, with the goal to pull back support as quickly as possible to promote independence.

Assessment. The paraprofessional plays an important role in measuring student progress by assisting and supporting teachers, especially with classroom logistics and student preparation. Paraprofessionals also are important sources of information on mastery. They collaborate with general and special educators to report progress they observe during their interactions with students. Paraprofessionals need to know and be able to articulate the difference between accommodations and modifications, and they must be able to clearly communicate to the team what level of support a student needed and was provided.

Communication. Paraprofessionals provide feedback to the teachers on the success of strategies used and make suggestions about possible improvements. They also assist the teachers in communicating with parents and families. Because paraprofessionals often implement strategies, accommodations, and modifications, it's common for families to direct questions about a student's progress to them. In order to ensure that the information given is consistent and accurate, paraprofessionals should refer such inquiries to the teachers.

Because they work in a variety of classrooms throughout the day, paraprofessionals also are responsible for maintaining effective and open communication with other school personnel. Although important information may be shared to facilitate effective supports, well-prepared paraprofessionals implement measures to protect the confidentiality of student information.

Leadership. Paraprofessionals work with all students in a classroom, including students with IEPs, and can have a great influence on their lives. Their presence can affect the social climate experienced by students with disabilities. The paraprofessional facilitates social relationships between students to allow natural supports to develop and friendships to evolve. Understanding the delicate nature of social situations among students and having the ability to fade from the scene whenever possible allow for these relationships to grow.

Paraprofessionals also demonstrate a leadership role when they create positive and reinforcing environments for students. It's work that increases learning and enhances performance among students and helps to build a school community in which students feel connected. Staff members who may be unfamiliar with a particular student can learn how to communicate or interact with him or her by observing the paraprofessional's general approach and specific strategies.

Record keeping. School and district procedures may require documentation of contact time for paraprofessionals assisting students with IEPs. Logs or time sheets should be current and accurate at all times. Clear roles and responsibilities of each educator reduce the gaps and avoid the duplications that might otherwise occur.

Establishing Schoolwide Inclusive Practices

Job descriptions alone do not create the symbiotic, collaborative atmosphere needed for this new vision of inclusive education to succeed. School leaders must work to create the conditions that enable staff to function as high-performing teams.

This begins by setting the tone of the school. School leaders identify the topics, activities, and processes that will be the staff's focus. In school after school, we have seen principal support for increased inclusion be the key to realizing the change. Of course, the teachers and staff have to implement the support systems, but the site administrator plays a pivotal role in creating and maintaining a vision of schoolwide inclusive practices (Villa & Thousand, 2016).

Administrators can guide policies on using the infused skills grid and lead decision making regarding under what conditions students receive instruction outside the general education classroom. They also develop and implement grading and assessment policies that support all students. Principals establish the culture of the school and clearly communicate the values and vision of the school as an inclusive learning place. To be effective, school leaders spend time in classrooms, too, observing but also offering guidance on instruction, assessment, accommodations, and modifications. And they hire the right people (those who are true believers in fully inclusive schools), provide incentives and support, and recognize the efforts and successes of their staff members to achieve their shared vision of inclusion.

We want to call out three more specific things school leaders can do to make this team-based approach to inclusion a reality.

Foster Collaboration Through Common Planning Time

Special and general educators need to have regularly scheduled contact with one another, even if they are not in a formal co-teaching arrangement. The knowledge educators possess about students and their progress is significant, but if there is no forum for sharing it, that knowledge is lost. School leaders of inclusive schools make it a priority to structure the master schedule to allow teachers time to plan together, and they include special educators in grade-level or content-area meetings.

The secondary school where three of us work places a high value on such interactions, assigning each teacher to two groups. The first is a grade-level group, in which general and special education teachers who share students come together for a deep dive about student academic progress. These conversations are not limited to paperwork; the teams make decisions about the best deployment of human and material resources for the coming week. For example, they collectively decide when the paraprofessional or special education teacher is needed in a particular classroom (e.g., a lab experiment in science, a test in mathematics). The second team to which each teacher belongs is content-specific; there is a history team, a science team, and so on. Special educators typically attend the content-specific department team meeting that aligns with their responsibilities. In addition, they meet as a special education team to focus on procedures that they have in common.

School leaders are the ones who make common planning time happen, and this may involve some creative use of personnel. For example, instructional coaches or other administrators (e.g., department heads) might "substitute" for special educators to enable them to attend grade-level meetings. Some schools hire a rotating substitute teacher to perform this function. It is important to note that these planning times should occur at regular intervals for a sustained period of time (at least one-hour increments), and all meetings should appear on the master schedule. This is part of an effective communication process and also allows teachers to anticipate when they will have time to collaborate.

Provide Appropriate Professional Learning Opportunities

Too often, administrators make assumptions about the interests of general or special education colleagues, relegating all support or intervention discussions to the special education faculty and failing to invite general educators to work as teacher leaders on such efforts. Special educators also need to continually develop their domain expertise if they are to adequately support the efforts of students with IEPs to master grade-level content. Supporting students in general education classrooms can be particularly challenging at the secondary level, as course mastery requires more technical knowledge. Even in the elementary grades, though, special educators deliver small-group instruction, re-teach, and develop accommodations for and modifications to activities and assessments. All of these practices are infinitely more difficult (if not impossible) when the content is not well understood by the special educator. Professional development for new curriculum, training about standards, and technical workshops should always include special educators working in the relevant disciplines. Of course, all professional development for general *and* special educators should mirror the best practices used daily in inclusive instructional environments:

- Focus on enhancing content knowledge and best practices in instruction.
- Address skills needed by everyone through supplemental instruction or intervention.
- Create opportunities for teachers to examine student data and collaborate.
- Provide teachers time to develop accommodations and modifications of lessons and strategies presented in the session.
- Ensure that follow-up instructional coaching includes both general and special educators.

Improve Accountability Systems

In some school systems, special education teachers are not directly accountable to the principal. Instead, they report to a district special education director, who is charged with evaluating teachers, renewing contracts, and overseeing job assignments. Although the principal is consulted, it is the district administrator who has the final word. These special educators are viewed as a resource for the district rather than the school. Some are itinerant teachers, and their job assignment may take them to more than one school site over the course of the week to provide services to students with low-incidence disabilities such as visual impairments. As a result, these teachers often are perceived as visitors, not fully engaged with the daily life of the school, and out of step with its culture and climate; they are an afterthought, without a mailbox or a name on the e-mail list for staff announcements.

If you are not a school administrator, principal, or teacher leader, circumstances like these may be out of your control—and even if you are in administration, your power to alter them will be limited. However, the following actions can support positive change:

- Identify by name all the itinerant teachers who work on your campus and make sure they have mailboxes, school identification, and some school "bling" with the school's name. These seemingly small details help people feel a part of your school community.
- Add the itinerant teachers to group e-mail messages and texts to keep them informed. They need to know, for example, when the entire 5th grade is going on a field trip, or when the staff will be celebrating the arrival of someone's new baby.
- Special education teachers who are at a school full-time but employed by another agency are likely to be supervised by someone outside your organization. Schedule quarterly meetings with such teachers to check in with them and find out what they need to do their job even better. In addition, schedule meetings with the teacher's direct supervisor so that you can reach consensus on goals.

Conclusion

Outdated thinking of discipline-specific roles in schools hinders efforts to realize a more inclusive environment that capitalizes on the collective expertise of the faculty. Department or grade-level meetings that do not include special educators reduce the likelihood that student needs will be addressed in a responsive manner. Responsiveness is further compromised when general and special educators lack the common planning time and professional learning that will foster collaboration. In addition, supervision models that assign special and general educators to different administrators, or that shift supervision to the district level, further distance special educators and related services providers from the flow of the school day. The divisions are further exacerbated when paraprofessionals are assigned to individual students as "shadows" or "one-on-one aides."

By redefining the roles of the adults, we can streamline and strengthen efforts to ensure that we go far beyond physically including students with disabilities in the general education classroom. Physical inclusion is basic. Purposefully promoting student independence, growth, authentic belongingness, and ultimate success—*this* has to be your aim as you shape and mold these roles as a school.

Changing Roles and Expectations

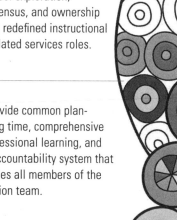

THE CHALLENGES

Separate special and general education departments subdivide human and fiscal resources.

Team members' roles in supporting students with disabilities are not clear, causing misunderstandings and creating overlap and gaps in instruction and services.

Traditional role divisions leave staff unprepared to take on the new roles and responsibilities of schoolwide inclusive practice.

THE SOLUTIONS

Redefine the roles and responsibilities of general education teachers, special education teachers, and paraprofessionals so that all share responsibility for instruction, assessment, communication, leadership, and record keeping.

Devote time to whole-school exploration, consensus, and ownership of the redefined instructional and related services roles.

Provide common planning time, comprehensive professional learning, and an accountability system that includes all members of the education team.

Download this graphic at www.ascd.org/ASCD/pdf/books/jung2019.pdf

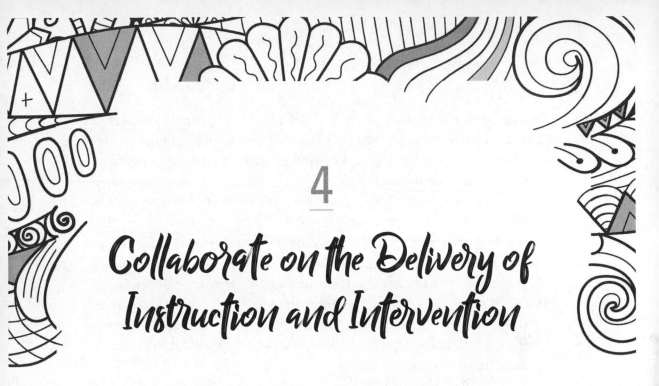

4

Collaborate on the Delivery of Instruction and Intervention

At Great Lakes Middle School, the 7th grade team was focused on building writing skills. A particular concern was that students with disabilities seemed trapped in a frustrating cycle. When they struggled with a writing assignment, they were sent to the resource room to get help: scaffolds and prompts from a special education teacher in one-on-one sessions. Their completed assignments went back to the general education teacher for a grade. Everyone on the team agreed that the process was effective in "saving the students from drowning" and that it enabled them to receive acceptable grades on their writing assignments. But was it actually helping students with disabilities develop as writers and master skills they could transfer to other work? The evidence suggested no. As time passed, writing did not get any easier for these students; they needed the same degree of help on assignment after assignment.

When teams use all of the special education service time to provide assistance with assignments, there is no time left—and often no people left—to teach *skills*. It's an approach that leaves special education teachers spinning their wheels, working long hours to create modifications for specific assignments that are neither planned nor recorded on performance measurements and are not accompanied by corresponding interventions or support strategies. As a support, it's a waste of the expertise special educators bring to the table.

Yes, educators want all students to perform well on tasks, assignments, activities, and assessments. But our real endgame is students developing the skills they need for a lifetime of happiness and success. Unless support or intervention empowers students and helps them advance along their chosen paths toward greater autonomy, it's creating a dependency. It does not build lifelong habits that matter to students, and it's an ineffective use of instructional time. "Help" given on assignments or homework that supplants time that could be spent on skill development is actually harm.

Early in her career, Nancy had a conversation with Margot, a special education teacher who was about to retire. Margot mentioned in passing the credentials she had earned throughout her career. Nancy was stunned to learn that when Margot completed her initial preparation program in the 1970s, she was able to add endorsements for autism, behavioral disorders, and intellectual disability by completing a single nine-week college course. When Nancy expressed surprise, Margot said, "But we knew so much less back then! I was studying to be a special education teacher right after they passed the law. All the content fit into one class."

The special education knowledge base has indeed exploded in the decades since the passing of landmark federal special education legislation in 1975. Yet ineffective and harmful models of service delivery like the one at Great Lakes Middle School linger in many schools, virtually unchanged. So what is the solution? As with all of the recommendations we make in this book, the answer lies not in special education or with a particular specialist or program or intervention strategy, but in a team working collaboratively in new ways.

Frameworks for Collaboration and Service Delivery

As we have previously discussed, instead of focusing on disability categories, educators need to focus on student needs and how to differentiate instruction and intervention. This naturally leads to a different approach to making placement decisions and meeting students' needs. Now, we want to delve deeper into how the roles of various educators within the school can complement one another as they work toward building the skills of everyone in the school—students and fellow teachers alike.

Special educators coordinate and deliver interventions to students who need them, working with general educators to monitor how students respond to the interventions that are provided and adjusting support along the way. Current best practices indicate that special educators should also spend more time purposefully building whole-school capacity by empowering the entire team—including peers—to effectively use a variety of instructional strategies and interventions.

Response to Intervention

Allison, a 16-year-old junior, has a reading-related disability and was struggling with her English 11 writing assignments. She also showed some difficulty with reading comprehension. At Allison's school, a response to intervention (RTI) framework is in place for making intervention decisions.

When Allison's IEP team met to discuss her evidence of learning in all areas, they determined that her slow reading pace and difficulty with academic language was holding her back. Because they had noticed that several other students could benefit from a boost in reading skills, they developed a plan to collaboratively deliver a short-term, small-group reading intervention using a station-teaching format. They decided that, for Allison, it made sense to cut one of the current semester's writing assignments so she could spend the time receiving additional reading intervention. In doing so, the team acknowledged that having a particular assignment score in the grade book was less important than Allison having a period of intensive intervention to increase her reading skills. The latter is an investment likely to pay off not only in terms of Allison's ability to complete future assignments in her classes at school but also in her life beyond school. It's an example a short-term intervention and support decision focused on long-term success.

Since the inception of RTI, there have been a number of myths and misconceptions surrounding it. Many people misunderstand RTI to mean that students at risk for failure should be removed from the general education setting and "put into RTI classrooms." If students don't make enough progress "in" RTI, they are referred for special education services. In other words, the tiers of RTI are misconceived as Tier 1 = general education classroom, Tier 2 = intervention classes for students who are failing, and Tier 3 = special education. It casts RTI as an intervention model for students who are failing and special education as the ultimate intervention.

However, RTI is and always was intended to be a prevention model, with remediation added only when excellent instruction is unsuccessful (Fletcher & Vaughn, 2009). With this mindset, teams constantly monitor students' potential for failure and consider students' response to the instruction as well as any interventions needed to ensure their learning and the learning of others (see Figure 4.1). RTI, then, is a whole-school, general education initiative aimed at systematically improving general education instruction in order to minimize the number of students who need intervention (Fisher & Frey, 2010).

What RTI means for general education is that the Tier 1 instruction all students receive is the focus of continuous improvement. Evidence-based strategies typically reserved for intervention become a proactive part of daily classroom activities, implemented as universal design for learning. If, for example, the data tell us that every year, a small group of students

Figure 4.1
RTI TIERS OF INTERVENTION

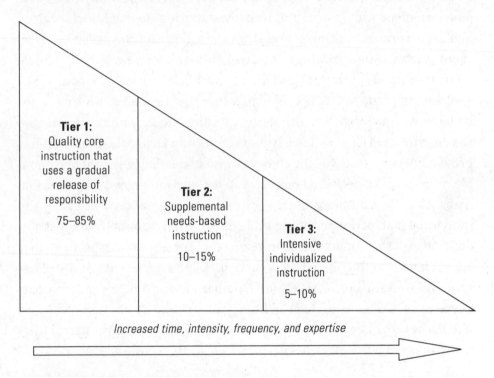

Tier 1:
Quality core
instruction that
uses a gradual
release of
responsibility

75–85%

Tier 2:
Supplemental
needs-based
instruction

10–15%

Tier 3:
Intensive
individualized
instruction

5–10%

Increased time, intensity, frequency, and expertise

Source: From *Enhancing RTI: How to Ensure Success with Effective Classroom Instruction and Intervention* (p. 23), by D. Fisher and N. Frey, 2010, Alexandria, VA: ASCD. Copyright 2010 by ASCD.

has difficulty with a concept or skill and benefits from supplemental intervention, the next time that concept or skill is taught, we will bring that successful intervention into the general education classroom and make it standard for *every student*. It's akin to the curb cuts in the sidewalk outside: necessary for those who use wheelchairs but also helpful to parents with strollers, roller skaters, delivery people with hand trucks, and cyclists. Excellent Tier 1 instruction means constantly looking for opportunities to make the curriculum accessible and effective for the broadest range of learners.

When 5th grade students had trouble planning and organizing their writing, Nicole, a special education teacher, would routinely pull them from language arts instruction to deliver writing intervention services. She used a graphic organizer and strategy instruction she designed to get them started. After working with these students for a few weeks, almost all of them had "gotten it" and didn't need her help any longer. Nicole and the 5th grade teacher decided together that instead of waiting to see which students might need the intervention, Nicole would bring it into the classroom (Tier 1) and teach all students how to use the tools that had previously been reserved for students who had failed. Over the next couple of weeks, she delivered large-group instruction on the graphic organizer. After that, both she and the 5th grade teacher used small-group and individual instruction in the general education classroom to support students' use of the organizers, monitoring their progress with performance data. Thanks to this proactive approach, only two students in the classroom needed further intervention, compared to seven or eight students in past years. These teachers did not wait to identify students who had failed; they *invested* in Tier 1 instruction first and saw the return on their investment in fewer students needing Tier 2 intervention.

MTSS: Casting a Wider Net

Effective practices for supporting every student continue to evolve. In this century, educators using RTI recognized that quality core instruction is crucial and precious intervention resources should not be needlessly expended as Band-Aids for poor Tier 1 practices (Fisher & Frey, 2010). In this decade, RTI practices have grown into increasingly comprehensive approaches to address students' behavioral needs and their social and emotional learning. These *multi-tiered systems of support* (MTSS) do not discriminate between those with and without IEPs. MTSS is a schoolwide process that provides specialized academic, behavioral, and emotional supports for any child who needs them. It can include access to counseling, instruction in self-regulation, supports for families, and instructional coaching to help more teachers provide better support for all students.

MTSS is a dynamic process built on the understanding that students must be able to flow in and out of intervention supports as needed. Therefore, assessment and progress monitoring—two hallmarks of RTI—are used to gauge progress and ensure that the process is responsive to student needs. If a student is stuck in a "Tier 2 intervention class" all semester or year because of scheduling, this isn't MTSS; this is inaccurate labeling of an older service delivery model (i.e., remedial education). However, school schedules are necessary, and it can be difficult to find the appropriate time to support students who need temporary intervention. Some schools have gone down the path of removing students from physical education, art, music, or other electives. But these classes are often ones that students enjoy the most or ones in which they have experienced some success. For students who have more significant needs, these classes may be where they feel truly included and enjoy a sense of belonging. Students who are already having a difficult time in school should never be put in a situation where they grow to dislike school even more.

American School Foundation in Monterrey, Mexico, arrived at a scheduling solution that has worked for many schools: instituting a "flex block" during the middle of the school day. During this block of time, any student can seek support from any teacher or counselor; they can also work independently. Within the online scheduling system, teachers can assign students to see a specific person during this time. In this model, for example, a student who is having trouble with a language arts assignment might spend time working on it alone, work on it with a peer, or visit the language arts teacher for strategic support.

Notably, with MTSS, students do not see an interventionist or special education teacher for help with assignments, because assignment help is not an intervention. A student struggling with a language arts assignment would go to the language arts teacher for help. Only students who seem to be having persistent difficulty with specific skills would work with a special educator, who would deliver a temporary, evidence-based intervention to help them build those skills. The duration of any intervention depends on the trajectory of the individual student's growth. Once a skill is gained, the skill-focused intervention concludes. If small-group intervention a few times a week is not enough to help a student gain the skill quickly, the school provides daily, more intensive intervention (i.e., Tier 3 intervention).

The effect of MTSS on school culture is that *all* students belong to *all* teachers. Tier 1 is the quality core instruction all students get. Intervention or intensive intervention is provided to any student who needs it, when they need it, and not for a day longer than they need it. Disability status is irrelevant in deciding if intervention is needed in an MTSS model. The goal of MTSS is ensuring that all students have access to high-quality instruction that is effective for them.

Sentencing students with disabilities to a segregated setting for part or all of the school day in effect presumes incompetence. MTSS, when delivered as intended, presumes competence: intervention is delivered immediately to any student who is at risk for failure. In this model, the general curriculum is not *replaced* with a lower-level curriculum; instead, students who are struggling get the general education instruction (Tier 1) *and* supplemental instruction or intervention to fill in gaps (Tier 2 or 3). Students are not placed in a generic catchall special education classroom; instead, they are selected for intervention purposefully to address a specific skill.

Co-Teaching: Capitalizing on Educator Knowledge

Even when it makes logical sense for the specialist to deliver the intervention, this does not necessarily mean that the student should be removed from general curriculum routines or activities. Through co-teaching, services are brought into the general education classroom using our "zone defense" structure: teachers help any student who needs support. General and special educators share responsibility for all students in the classroom;

teaching, re-teaching, paperwork, and progress monitoring are not solely the responsibility of one or the other, and neither are the students.

Instances of co-teaching exist in a rapidly growing number of schools, with the stated purpose of the arrangement being to serve students with disabilities in the least restrictive environment and expand the reach of intervention to other learners who need support. Co-teaching is key to getting students with disabilities out of segregated, separate settings. It offers the extra hands in the room to make this feasible as well as additional brainpower to solve problems and generate ideas.

We recognize that co-teaching has a limited impact on learning; according to Hattie (2012), it has an effect size of .19, well below the average effect of .40. However, based on a review of the studies included in Hattie's meta-analyses, we believe this is because most implementations of co-teaching are flawed. When we ask teachers what they think of when they hear "co-teaching," a common response is that the specialist is in the general education classroom, the general education teacher is delivering a lesson, and the specialist is helping as needed with a student or group of students. *That is not co-teaching.* It's simple applying the name *co-teaching* to a co-support model. The fact that there is more than one educator working in the same classroom does not mean these educators are co-teaching. We hypothesize that high-quality co-teaching models, such as those we will discuss in the paragraphs that follow, have a much higher impact on student learning. Furthermore, there are impacts on *adult* learning that would not be possible without co-teaching.

In true co-teaching there is co-planning, co-instruction, co-assessment, and co-reflection. The general and special educator trade lead and supporting roles as needed. This dynamic and fluid practice requires that both teachers possess strong communication skills and have opportunities to problem solve. Scruggs and Mastropieri (2017) point out, "It is *what* the two teachers do and *how* they do it that can make co-teaching effective for students with disabilities" (p. 285). This is what makes clear role and responsibility agreements, like those detailed in Chapter 3, so crucial.

Although the discussion of co-teaching has often centered around the concept of improving outcomes of students with learning differences in general education classrooms, the benefits of co-teaching can have other far-reaching effects. Special and general educators learn from one another; special educators gain skills in the general curriculum, and general educators gain research-based interventions they can implement on a regular basis within the general education classroom. Because of the transactional effect of teaming, co-teaching not only helps the targeted students (through the planned learning experience) but also results in long-term, permanent improvement in the quality of core instruction. Purposeful design of these capacity-building experiences is necessary to maximize their potential.

The implications of role release—using consultative service delivery to provide adult support—are significant and also require careful planning. Before releasing a role, create systematic supports so that the person taking it on is more likely to succeed. In Chapter 2, we talked about how deciding on the right frequency and intensity of services is largely a matter of figuring out how much support other adults need to implement an intervention. The benefits of co-teaching can be maximized, then, by asking for each lesson, "What is the purpose of each educator in the room, both in terms of supporting students and in supporting each other's learning?"

There is not just a single method of co-teaching; in fact, Friend and Cook (2007) have identified seven models with a range of different benefits. In a team-based approach to co-teaching, both teachers have a role in determining the best model to use based on the purpose of instruction, the composition of the classroom, and the skills and strengths of each of the teachers.

These seven models are not static, and teaching partners do not need to adhere to only one. In fact, we counsel teams to expand their instructional repertoire over time to encompass all seven. However, the shared vocabulary of distinct models allows teams to communicate clearly about which approach(es) they will be using during a lesson or unit, and for what purpose. As we have stated many times, effective communication is key.

Let's look at the models one by one.

One Teach, One Assist

In this model of co-teaching, one teacher has the primary responsibility for carrying out the teaching for the lesson. The second teacher assists in a purposeful and planned way.

One teach, one assist contrasts from the traditional assistance model in two important ways. First, in this and all models of co-teaching, both teachers are involved in planning, delivery of instruction, and assessment of learning. There is no hierarchy in this approach, where one teacher is more important than the other. Second, the "assistance" does not mean a teacher is assigned to a particular student to help in whatever way needed. Instead, assistance is carefully planned and may be directed to a particular student, delivered to a certain area of the classroom, or—if it relates to a particular skill—delivered to all students needing that assistance.

For example, Monica Taylor is engaged in a shared reading with her 4th grade students. She reads the text aloud, sharing her thinking. Tiffany Gaspar, a special education teacher, visits with specific students as the class listens to Ms. Taylor read. Sometimes Ms. Gaspar redirects students, and other times she adds clarifying information. During this 20-minute part of the literacy block, Ms. Gaspar is assisting in the class. At other times, she takes a leading role.

Station Teaching

Although *station teaching* is more often used in early childhood classrooms, it is appropriate for use at any grade. In this model, there are two or more areas of the classroom where students spend time. Students are divided into small groups, and these groups of students rotate among the

stations. Stations can be facilitated by a teacher or designed for independent navigation (e.g., a classroom might have two stations where students
work on a particular concept with instructors and a third station where
students practice a skill independently).

Station teaching is an effective way to provide small-group instruction
on more difficult concepts. It also offers an opportunity to differentiate
by selecting and assigning particular stations for students. Students who
have mastered a concept, for example, may be sent to an independent station, while those who need additional instruction could be assigned to a
facilitated one. The class in our example, offering three stations during
the class period, might assign students to visit two of the three.

Following their whole-class lesson each day, the students in Arturo
Garcia's algebra class move to their learning stations. One station focuses
on online practice; students do this work independently. Another station
is led by Mr. Garcia, who guides students through the conceptual thinking
behind the problems they solve together. Another station is led by Marisol
Ruiz, a special educator, who has students think aloud as they solve problems so that she can identify errors in their processes. Over the course of
the period, all students visit each station.

Parallel Teaching

The *parallel teaching* model involves two teachers in the same classroom, each instructing half of the students. There is no difference in what
is being taught or the teaching methods used.

The primary advantage of parallel teaching is the resulting smaller
instructional groups. Smaller groups allow for more dialogue and afford
teachers a clearer understanding of where individual students are in their
learning. This model can also be useful if there are significant behavior
challenges, or if the content is new or difficult. In fact, any time teachers
feel a lower student-to-teacher ratio would be beneficial, parallel teaching is a reasonable consideration.

In a co-taught middle school English class, students are divided into two groups for close reading lessons. The text selected is very complex, and the two teachers in this class know that they can support students' thinking better by reducing the student-teacher ratio for this task. Both groups have the same text and work to answer the same questions in a think-pair-share arrangement. All students still talk with their partners about the questions asked, but each teacher has fewer students to observe and thus more time to devote to listening and follow-up.

One Teach, One Observe

In the *one teach, one observe* model of co-teaching, one teacher takes the lead in delivering instruction, and the other teacher spends time in purposeful observation. The observing teacher may be observing the instruction, student learning, or behavior. Take, for example, a general and special education co-teaching pair in which the special educator has an instructional strategy she would like to try in the classroom. The general educator serves in the observer role in order to see the new strategy in action and learn how to use it. The roles could then switch, with the general educator implementing the new strategy and the special educator observing to check for fidelity of the new strategy and provide formative feedback to the general educator.

This model is an ideal choice for teachers to share and learn from one another to build capacity. We should choose this option often! Observation can also be used to collect data on student learning or behavior. Through this co-teaching model, the first teacher can devote attention to the instruction, knowing that the second teacher is collecting the data needed to make future instructional decisions.

Mary Wexford watches her kindergarten students think each day when the special education teacher, Heidi Shaw, leads the learning. Ms. Wexford explained, "When you're leading the learning, it's hard to observe the learning and figure out where students are getting stuck. Having Ms. Shaw teach and me observe allows us to decide what we need to do in the small-group instruction that will come later." Ms. Shaw also gets a chance to observe as Ms. Wexford teaches, but her focus is typically on the students with identified disabilities. Ms. Shaw said, "I like to get a sense of how well our supports are working. I watch to see how students are responding to the instruction and to their peers. This helps me figure out how I can continually adjust the supports to get better learning outcomes for our students."

Supplemental Teaching

The *supplemental teaching* model has one teacher in the co-teaching pair focusing on students who are struggling with a concept or skill and need additional instruction or intervention. Although supplemental teaching differs from other co-teaching models in that the two teachers may not be in the same room during delivery, it is still a necessary part of the continuum and it is still co-teaching: both teachers take part in the planning, delivery, and assessment.

A key feature of supplemental instruction is that it never *replaces* the general curriculum instruction. If a student needs support in writing, that student is not pulled from writing instruction to receive intervention; the student receives the writing instruction from the first teacher as a part of the general curriculum *and* receives intervention from the second teacher.

One of the decisions teams need to make to deliver this type of co-teaching is *when* the supplemental instruction will be delivered. Teams should select times when students are engaged in independent work or learning centers. Another consideration for supplemental instruction is how long to continue providing it. Students should receive the supplemental instruction only as long as it is needed. This model of co-teaching is effective for teaching specific skills to students who need those skills. Once the student has gained the skill, supplemental instruction on that skill should cease.

There are several students in Maxine Baker's 1st grade class who have unfinished learning when it comes to sound-symbol correspondence. The majority of the class is reading decodable texts as part of their small-group learning. While they work independently or in centers, the students who need to learn the sounds for individual letters and blends meet with the special educator, Thom Harper. Students who need assistance with onset and rime patterns meet with Ms. Baker. Through supplemental teaching, Ms. Baker and Mr. Harper provide targeted skill development to help every student develop his or her literacy skills.

Alternative Teaching

Alternative teaching involves two teachers delivering the same content but using different methods. The class is divided into two groups, and each group receives the instruction from both teachers—first one, then the other.

Like parallel teaching, this approach carries the advantage of students learning in smaller instructional groups. But unlike parallel teaching, teachers use different instructional methods or strategies, in effect giving students double exposure to the content. This model is based on the theory that the teaching methods that are effective for one student may not be the most effective methods for another student. The calculation is that by using both methods for the full group, fewer students will need supplemental instruction.

The co-teachers of U.S. History II at Panhandle High School like to test instructional methods to see which is more effective for their students. For example, during a unit on the political, social, economic, technological, and cultural developments of the 1920s, they identified different strategies they wanted to try for teaching the same set of academic vocabulary words. Kayla Thibodeau, the special educator, used a vocabulary self-collection tool with one half of the class, while Tabitha Hanson used word cards with the other. These teachers knew that both approaches had strong evidence of effectiveness, but they decided to present the vocabulary acquisition as a competition, each telling their respective groups that their strategy was better and that the students would be able to prove it.

Team Teaching

Team teaching was described by Friend and Cook (2007) as the most advanced form of co-teaching. Although they presented it as a distinct model, it can also be thought of as the ideal execution of a number of models used in combination. In other words, team teaching is what is delivered by pairs of teachers who have worked together for years and have a deep understanding of each other's instructional strengths and styles of teaching. To an observer, it is not apparent who is the general educator and who is the special educator. Students, if asked, may not be able to identify the "main" teacher, because both teachers have equal roles and multiple means of delivering co-taught lessons.

Regardless of the model used for collaboration and co-teaching, the adults in the classroom must have a common language of instruction from which to plan learning. They draw on a shared understanding of what constitutes high-quality instruction as they plan and implement learning experiences that build student competence and confidence. Without this shared framework, co-teachers can be at odds with each other, and students will suffer. Our experience and research suggests that the gradual release of responsibility framework is structured enough to support shared understanding of instructional moves but flexible enough to allow teachers room to innovate.

The GRR Framework: Providing Common Ground for Effective Instruction

You've heard it countless times: *good teaching is good teaching.* For nearly two decades, Doug and Nancy have studied the characteristics and effectiveness of a gradual release of responsibility (GRR) instructional framework (see Fisher & Frey, 2014a). This model has its roots in reading comprehension and was first described in 1983 by Pearson and Gallagher, who articulated a theory of textual understanding that includes read-alouds, shared reading, guided reading, and independent reading. Their theory was then widely applied as a path for reading instruction.

However, some students failed to make progress despite teachers' good-faith efforts. Examination of the model led Doug and Nancy to the realization that the missing component was *collaborative learning*. They expanded the instructional framework across the curriculum, from elementary through high school (see Figure 4.2). They examined the responsiveness of English learners, students identified as high-achieving, students at risk of school failure, and students with IEPs. In all scenarios, classroom instruction improved, and student learning increased (Fisher & Frey, 2003; Fisher, Frey, & Lapp, 2011).

Here is a condensed look at the four phases of the gradual release of responsibility model.

Figure 4.2
THE GRADUAL RELEASE OF RESPONSIBILITY INSTRUCTIONAL FRAMEWORK

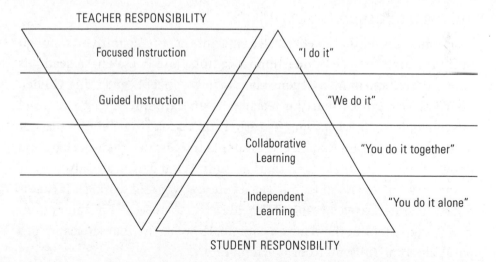

Source: From *Better Learning Through Structured Teaching: A Framework for the Gradual Release of Responsibility,* 2nd ed. (p. 3), by D. Fisher and N. Frey, 2014, Alexandria, VA: ASCD. Copyright 2014 by ASCD.

Focused Instruction: "I Do It."

In this phase of instruction, the teacher assumes the majority of the cognitive and metacognitive demand. Focused instruction on the part of the teacher should include communicating the lesson's purpose for learning (sometimes called the *learning intention* or *learning target*). Students deserve to know the relevance of what they are learning; telling them, "Because there's a test next Friday" is not building relevance. Nor does the "purpose" have to be something that leads to world peace. However, when children hear that learning syllables makes it easier to spell, or that being able to calculate slope in mathematics is similar to what skateboarders mentally do when they take a ramp, they have more interest and more reason to learn.

During focused instruction, the teacher may use modeling and thinking aloud to share expert thinking with students. *Modeling* demonstrates for students how they might engage with content, and it illustrates how an expert applies concepts and skills. *Thinking aloud* brings students inside this decision-making process.

Guided Instruction: "We Do It."

In this phase, the teacher releases some of the cognitive responsibility through the use of questions, prompts, and cues. These scaffolds allow students to immerse themselves in new concepts and skills. Guided instruction requires that the teacher listen carefully for and redirect misconceptions but *not* jump in with a correction. Instead, the teacher might ask a question that directs students to consider their background knowledge ("Let's think about that carefully. What do you already know is always true of a parallelogram? Does your answer still work?"). If that is not sufficient, the teacher might provide a cue to overtly shift their attention ("Take a look at the chart on page 32. How are the characteristics of a parallelogram different from a rectangle?").

Collaborative Learning: "You Do It Together."

In this phase, students work together to consolidate their understanding, and in doing so, they use the academic language and the disciplinary thinking and reasoning associated with the subject. Working through a collaborative task exposes students to their own partial understandings, too. How often have you thought you understood something only to discover, when you tried to do it, that there were gaps in your knowledge? The collaborative phase of learning ensures that students aren't set adrift, trying to figure things out on their own.

There are a number of ways to facilitate collaborative learning, such as jigsaws, reciprocal teaching, and think-pair-share. Consider, for example, when the students in Maria Gonzalez's class are creating a poster to show what they know about fossils, with each student using an assigned-color marker to make his or her contribution. They are talking with one another, sharing ideas, and then adding to the poster in writing—and creating a record of their individual input to group output.

Independent Learning: "You Do It Alone."

In the independent learning phase, students apply what they have learned and ask themselves new questions about the topic, undertaking authentic tasks and producing products. This is a time when students are deliberatively practicing what they have been learning.

There are three purposes for independent learning, and the task should be driven by the intent:

- Fluency building to develop automaticity and promote retrieval of information
- Application in different contexts to promote transfer of learning
- Spiral review to revisit skills or concepts acquired earlier in the year to address challenges associated with new content

GRR Misconceptions and the Repercussions

There are several misconceptions about GRR that are important to address. First, it is not a framework that is scripted and rigid and that must be followed in a lockstep manner. A lesson might easily begin with independent learning (bell work posted on the board), followed by guided instruction (debriefing the bell work, as the teacher listens for misconceptions and scaffolds thinking). The lesson might then shift to focused learning (sharing the purpose for the lesson and providing direct instruction and modeling) with additional guided instruction, before moving on to collaborative learning as students apply skills in small groups. During the group work, the teacher might be circulating to provide on-the-spot guided instruction to groups that have stalled, before wrapping up the lesson with independent learning in the form of a written or drawn exit slip.

Another misconception is that all four types of learning are not necessary components in every lesson—that is to say, it's fine if today's lesson doesn't include any independent learning if tomorrow's will. With the exception of a testing situation in which no teaching is occurring, all four phases of the GRR framework need to be present in every lesson. Ask yourself these questions:

- Is there ever a lesson in which students don't deserve to know what they are learning?
- Can you conceive of a worthwhile lesson in which you wouldn't need to scaffold students' understanding?
- Should students ever be denied the chance to learn with peers because you didn't get around to preparing discussion prompts or planning collaborative tasks?
- Would there ever be a case in which learners wouldn't benefit from practicing a newly taught skill?

When any GRR phase is omitted because it's viewed as optional, it's the vulnerable students in the class who pay the steepest price. All four instructional moves are crucial for all learners, but especially so for those who are not yet making expected progress. The way to accelerate learning is to create the conditions that allow learning to occur.

Conclusion

It's hard to be part of a team when you behave as if you are a solo act. Arndt and Liles (2010) call this the "separate spheres framework" (p. 15); it's the "You do your job, and I'll do mine" mindset. Collaboration is key to the success of inclusive classrooms. Co-teaching models allow more students to experience more success because they have access to more expertise. Students without disabilities enjoy a number of incidental benefits when they are prompted, cued, and questioned by a knowledgeable special educator. And students with disabilities benefit by accessing content expertise with appropriate support.

In addition, RTI/MTSS and the GRR framework provide general and special education teachers with a structure for working productively with one another. As we discussed in Chapter 3, instituting truly inclusive practices requires redefining the roles and responsibilities of educators. We have stressed in this chapter that educators need to collaborate and that there are systems that allow this new team dynamic to flourish. These systems allow an instructional team to focus on each student's needs, providing quality instruction and interventions as needed. Importantly, it is the means to the ends we really seek, which is for all students to develop skills and habits that they can use beyond the classroom rather than simply earning passing scores on the tasks they are assigned.

Changing the Team Dynamic

THE CHALLENGES

Students with disabilities receive instruction within a general education setting but through a restrictive service delivery model.

The school relies on one-on-one paraprofessional support to help students participate.

Special education teachers in "inclusive" classrooms are relegated to an assistant role, with general education teachers responsible for most instruction, communication with families, and student assessment and grading.

Interventions and supports focus on task completion.

Instruction is fragmented and piecemeal. The gradual release of responsibility model is not implemented regularly.

THE SOLUTIONS

Have classroom teachers use service delivery models that include group support along with individual support to realize benefits for all students, with and without disabilities.

Have paraprofessionals promote the natural support of classmates to provide opportunities for students to grow academically.

Use a "zone defense" framework to ensure support is provided to any student who needs it. Employ a variety of co-teaching models to build capacity in all teachers and limit interventions that remove students from general education classroom.

Focus interventions and supports on the skills students need to develop.

Design learning for all students using the gradual release of responsibility model. Vary the order of the phases to ensure that learning expectations are met.

5

Honor Student Aspirations and Plan Accordingly

Kelly told the team of professionals assembled to help her identify her educational goals for the coming year that she wanted to be a police officer.

"Well, you're only in 8th grade," one of the team members said. "It's a little early to think about that."

Another said, "It's good to have dreams, Kelly, but we need to focus on reality."

A third team member said, "Kelly, you have Down syndrome, and it's just not physically possible for you to be a police officer. Let's talk about career goals that will fit with your skills."

That was when Kelly's mom ended the meeting. She removed Kelly from that school and went shopping for a new one that wasn't so eager to shut down her daughter's dreams.

Fast-forward to Kelly's senior year. She had an internship working at the front counter of a local police substation. She answered calls and assisted in the office and with the officers. The team at Kelly's new school had figured out how help her pursue her dreams. After graduation, the police department hired Kelly to work in communications. We don't know if she will become a police officer herself. What we do know is that she is a very happy young woman who gets to interact with officers and contribute to the safety of her community.

People start dreaming about their future careers and the lives they want to live in early childhood. Given that, we wonder why planning for the transition to life after high school is seldom a focus until high school. What if educators prompted students to talk about and explore their aspirations at an earlier age? Would this affect their interest and engagement in school? Would they graduate from high school better prepared to follow their dreams? What would their outcomes be later in life? In this chapter, we will look at what it means, and what it takes, to honor students' aspirations.

A Need for IEP Reform

We have said already that students with disabilities don't have "special needs"; they have special *rights*. You could effectively argue that every student deserves an individualized education plan or at least an opportunity to clarify who and what they want to be. But for students with disabilities enrolled in U.S. public schools, this process is mandatory. The whole idea of the IEP goal-setting process is to identify a student's aspirations and then identify the learning they need to realize those dreams.

Carla walked into the IEP meeting unsure of what to expect. Her son, Jalen, was in 3rd grade and had been recently diagnosed with a learning disability. The special education teacher greeted everyone and began by reading Jalen's test score results. She then discussed the interventions that had been put in place. Before Carla could get her bearings and understand the flow of the meeting, the special education coordinator was reading the goals she'd written for Jalen's IEP. There was one about reading skills (fluency and decoding multisyllabic words) and another about reading comprehension. Carla hadn't been in an IEP meeting before and it all felt very foreign to her, including the formal and legal language that was being used to describe Jalen. It wasn't clear to Carla what her role was, but she signed the documents and agreed to the services. The team of professionals surely knew best.

The IEP process has drifted far from the intent of the droves of parents who stormed Washington, D.C., in the 1970s demanding services for their children with disabilities. The heart of the IEP process and the meetings that accompany it should be aspirational goal setting, shared plan development, meaningful problem solving, and individualization. But IEP meetings so easily slip into a 60-minute sterile litany of numbers and legalese, capped with a formulaic review of goals and objectives. In reality, few IEP teams dig deep to get to what really matters to the student and will support that student's growth and development, provide access to the general education curriculum, and set the stage for a fulfilling life. Further, the inattention to student and family aspirations in effect creates an inequitable education for young people with disabilities. Rather than receiving a coherent educational experience that provides the tools students need to achieve their dreams, they are subjected to a fragmented experience with a revolving door of educators. We cannot imagine a student, with or without disabilities, being able to easily reach his or her dreams in an inequitable school.

Honor Student Voice

For many families, the IEP meeting experience means walking into a conversation that has started without them. The adult educators sit around the table and review goals that have already been drafted. Having provided no input (it wasn't asked for), the family is unprepared to do little more than agree or disagree with the predetermined goals. Although students should be an active part of their IEP meetings, many students—especially younger ones—aren't even present. When they are invited to their IEP meetings, they often find themselves in the role of a nonparticipant observer, sitting in a room filled with adults in positions of power over them discussing what they need. Student input, when it's asked for, might be limited to answering a few questions posed by the team. Most students show up and simply agree with the teachers' goals and plan. But how can students be expected to meet a goal if they don't know what the goal is, if they have no sense of ownership of it, or if it isn't relevant to them? *Whose goals are these, anyway?* Goals are something we should develop *with* students instead of *for* them.

Lee Ann didn't think twice about inviting her 2nd grade son to one of his first IEP meetings; *of course* he would be there! But the team seemed surprised to see him, and the meeting moved forward awkwardly, with most of the adults clearly uncomfortable speaking about the little boy's disabilities and goals. But the little boy had a lot to add. He had opinions on the spelling technology they wanted to use (he didn't like it and wanted to learn to use a dictionary instead), and he had reflections on how visual strategies worked well for him. He ended up with a goal about Dolch sight words and another about oral reading fluency. Both were fine goals, but Lee Ann's son also wanted to read a Harry Potter book by himself one day, and he wanted to learn how to build computers. His team would have known this had they given him the opportunity to provide input beforehand.

Why are some teams reluctant to invite younger students to their IEP meetings? Does a kindergarten or 1st grade student have nothing to add? Is the reasoning that telling students they have a disability will damage their confidence? The truth of the matter is that students are not ignorant of their abilities and challenges simply because no one has specifically talked to them about their needs. Believe us, students who qualify for an IEP feel their differences whether or not anyone acknowledges them. In fact, not talking about their needs or disability may only serve to bring shame—and need for support or the identification of disability should not be something for which any student ever feels embarrassment or shame. It's time for the forgotten student voice to return and be visible in every IEP and in every classroom. IEPs are to be done *with* students and *for* students, not *to* them.

Begin with the End in Mind

At IEP and similar meetings around the world, teams often start with the present level of performance, with goals emerging from the needs highlighted in the present-level review. Where is the student in all of this? Students don't benefit when they are only described in terms of their grades and what they can't do. It's virtually impossible to get at what really matters to a student and set in motion a life-altering plan when a deficit model is the default mode. Their hopes, dreams, likes, dislikes, and passions should have far more weight than their test scores.

Educators are called to "begin with the end in mind" as we use backward design to create curriculum and assessments. This is exactly what's called for when we develop an IEP with a student and family. The IEP process should begin, well in advance of the formal IEP meeting, by asking the student and family to share their priorities and dreams for the future. This can't be window dressing; the answers need to reach the IEP *before* goals are drafted. Remember, the IEP meeting is only where the IEP is finalized, but the process begins weeks in advance, with families and students as driving forces every step of the way.

When you think about the IEP meetings you've been a part of recently, did it feel like the culmination of a family-and-student-driven process? Would you describe the plans discussed as connected to a life-changing outcome that the student and family articulated in advance? Did those dreams shape the IEP and inform the annual goals? Or would you say the IEP stopped short of this ideal and merely achieved legal compliance?

Educators can look to person-centered planning practices as an alternative to the status quo. This approach involves leveraging the collective wisdom of teachers, family members, and a wide network of supporters. The idea is to fully engage the student's support network in articulating new possibilities. The person-centered planning process helps fine-tune student dreams and aspirations, while also identifying ways that the people who care about the students can support them in accomplishing their goals.

One tool to support this process is Making Action Plans—MAPs for short (O'Brien, Pearpoint, & Kahn, 2010). MAPs provides a platform for students to dive deeper into their aspirations and elicit help and guidance from those closest to them. Although the discussion is facilitated by an adult, it is led by the student and takes place before the IEP meeting. Its purpose is to find out what outcomes would help the student reach his or her ultimate dream so that educators can work backward to figure out what must be done now to move the student toward that future.

The other participants in the MAPs process should be the student's "fan base"—anyone who is a part of the student's life, cares about him or her, and can invest in supporting the plan. Some members of this team may invest a great deal of resources and time, while others play a supporting, but still significant, role. During the meeting, everyone discusses the student's history, family, dreams, gifts and talents, and current needs in a personal and informal atmosphere. This conversation weaves together the perspectives of everyone involved to paint a picture of the student's experiences (good and bad) up to this point in time. This is a chance to celebrate the story that makes the student unique and what his or her interests are right now, and begin thinking about the supports the student will need to pursue passions, interests, and dreams. The team talks through the evolution of the dream, and as is the case for many of us, it often connects back to an experience or interaction at an early age. Whereas discussions at IEP meetings can often be formal and legal, MAPs discussions are designed to be conversational and organic. The process is documented not on forms but with colorful visuals on chart paper or a whiteboard.

Set Goals That Support the Dream

Consider the following IEP goal:

> By annual review, [student's name] will utilize planning skills by creating a timeline (to complete each step of a multistep task) in order to complete task in time provided (including using extended time he is allowed) and self-monitor for correctness

> using rubrics/checklist (in writing) and calculator (in math) to
> check for accuracy of work before submitting for a grade on 9
> out of 10 trials.

This was an actual goal Lee Ann found while reviewing middle school IEPs in 2017. Nothing in this goal reveals anything about the student—or an intended outcome. In the midst of the IEP team's attempt to cover *everything*, the student was lost. As Lee Ann flipped the pages of plan after plan, all of the goals for this school looked pretty much like this one.

Research on IEP quality confirms that this school wasn't an outlier. IEP goals are often difficult to understand, measure, and support (see Ruble, McGrew, Dalrymple, & Jung, 2010). Sadly, goals are often so generic that students end up having the same goals year after year. Or goals are not specific to a student, and every student supported by a given special educator has essentially the same goals. Goals also tend to be written in ways that are discipline driven—there are the "speech goals," the "PT goals," the "special educator's goals," and so on. We are often left wondering, "Where are the *kid's* goals?" The reality is that many IEP meetings are much more about satisfying the legal requirements for documentation than crafting meaningful plans for students. In an effort to meet the letter of the law, IEPs have morphed into 30- and 40-page legal documents that completely miss the point. What makes a goal meaningful? In our view, a meaningful goal is one that has the potential to change the student's life.

Alex, a 17-year-old junior, is interested in auto body work after high school and has spent the past few years working at his uncle's welding business, learning the skill of automotive welding. Anthony Carter, Alex's welding teacher, and Simone Davila, his special education teacher, met with Alex and his mom to begin thinking about Alex's IEP and transition goals for the coming year. After listening to Alex describe his dream to have his own auto body shop, Mr. Carter reflected, "Alex, last year you said you wanted to work for your uncle after graduation. Now you're wanting to extend that toward an ultimate goal of having your own auto body business. This is ambitious, and I know you will be a successful business owner. You're hardworking and driven and have really come into your own this year! So it seems we have a clear direction for a goal after high school. You do still need to earn a welding certificate, like we've talked about in class. You are still planning to work part-time for your uncle while you earn that?"

Alex didn't hesitate. "Yeah, I need to start making money after graduation to save for my business." Alex's mom added, "And you'd get to practice what you're learning about welding at the shop."

"Great," Ms. Davila said. "Then you want to set a goal of staying employed part-time at your uncle's shop to save money—maybe work 15 to 20 hours a week. You want to earn a welding certificate, and ultimately, you want to have your own successful auto body shop. Does that sum it up?"

Alex agreed that it did, and Mr. Carter then turned the conversation to what Alex needed to accomplish over the next year to further his pursuit of these goals. "You know, Alex," Mr. Carter said, "if you want to be a business owner, maybe you want to take some of the business classes we have here. Mrs. Tutweiller is an excellent teacher, and everyone in her class works on learning how to make a business plan."

"That sounds pretty cool!" Alex said in an interested and upbeat way.

Ms. Davila added, "And there are four or five other business classes. For some people, business is their main program here. You have real leadership skills, and I think you'd really like what these have to offer."

"I could get into that," Alex said.

Mr. Carter shared an idea: "What about making the completed business plan your goal for school over the next year?"

"That sounds good to me," replied Alex.

Mr. Carter returned to a goal from a previous plan. "Now, it's hard for me to imagine, but you used to have a goal for managing your frustration and anger. I've not seen you have one hint of difficulty with this in my class, but how do you feel about your ability to keep your cool at work? You can't lose it on the job. You'd get fired."

"Yeah, or lose customers," Alex added. "I know I need to work on not getting so mad. And I'm not sure what it would be like interacting with a customer who made me angry. I guess I need to think about that."

"Yes, dealing with the public can be really frustrating," Mr. Carter said. "Even when you're right, you have to make the customer happy. That's hard for anyone."

"OK," Ms. Davila said. "Since you want to work on ways to interact professionally with customers and bosses at work, we could write a goal about that to get you ready for the cranky customers you'll eventually have to be nice to." Alex agreed this was a good idea, and he, his teachers, and his mom worked together to write goals that were clear to everyone.

Planning for Goal Attainment

Setting goals that feed into students' aspirations is only the beginning of the journey. In order to ensure that quality core instruction and specialized supports are helping students attain their goals, teachers need to monitor student progress and provide necessary support and redirection. The problem is, IEPs rarely include sufficient detail for everyone on the team to know exactly what to do to support goal attainment and how to measure progress toward success.

This gap between the big picture and the everyday can be bridged by developing a *goal attainment scale* for each goal (Cytrynbaum, Ginath, Birdwell, & Brandt, 1979). A goal attainment scale is a ruler of sorts for measuring progress on any personalized or individualized goal. Goal attainment scales help teachers measure student progress simply and quickly in the context of everyday routines and activities. Figure 5.1 provides an example.

Lee Ann was first introduced to goal attainment scaling as a researcher working on a National Institutes of Health–funded study of an intervention for students with autism (Ruble, McGrew, Toland, Dalrymple, & Jung, 2013). Through her work, Lee Ann realized that this process should

Figure 5.1
SAMPLE GROWTH PLAN

Growth Plan for Alyssia   **Start Date:** 16-Jan

Annual Goal		Settings			
During language arts, social studies, art, and science, I will persist in writing and drawing tasks for at least 20 minutes without discomfort or frustration for 5 days in a row.		a language arts b social studies c art d science			

Scale			Data				
Goal	4	20 minutes or more	Date	a	b	c	d
	3.5		16-Jan	0			
Benchmark 3	3	15 minutes	18-Jan		0	0	
	2.5		30-Jan	0			0
Benchmark 2	2	10 minutes	6-Feb		0.5	1	
	1.5		13-Feb	0.5		0.5	2.5
Benchmark 1	1	5 minutes	27-Feb	1	1		
	0.5		2-Mar			1.5	1
Baseline	0	3 minutes or less	9-Mar	0			

Strategies

What Alyssia will do: *I will use my adapted pencil and will make sure I'm comfortable before I start. If I need a break, I'll take a 3-minute break and start again.*

What environmental changes are needed: An adapted pencil, calming background music when possible. Check Alyssia's chair to see if an adjustment is needed.

What others will do within the general curriculum: Use a 4-minute timer to show Alyssia how long she needs to write or draw. Once she draws for 4 minutes without becoming fatigued or frustrated, show her the data map of progress and ask her how it feels to have accomplished this. After she has met this criterion 10 times in a row, change the criterion to increase by 1 minute. Continue changing the criterion until she reaches 20 minutes, showing her progress regularly.

Additional intensive interventions needed: None

Date	a	b	c	d
12-Mar		0.5	2	0.5
28-Mar			2.5	1
6-Apr	1.5		1.5	
13-Apr		2		
23-Apr	0.5	1.5		1.5
1-May			0.5	
9-May	2	2.5		3
18-May			2	
25-May				2.5
27-Aug	2.5	2.5	3	
5-Sep		3	3	2.5
20-Sep	3			
4-Oct			3	
15-Oct	4	3	3	3.5
29-Oct	2.5	3.5		3
1-Nov	0.5		1	
13-Nov		2.5	3	
29-Nov	3		3.5	3
5-Dec		3.5		
17-Dec	3.5			3.5
4-Jan		4	4	
14-Jan	4			4

not be reserved for research; it should be a part of the daily work in every classroom when measuring growth on the skills that matter the most to students.

We must stress that goal attainment scaling is a personalized and individualized process; teachers and IEP teams should use whatever measure makes the most sense for the goal. For example, if a student wants to persist in reading longer, then duration measured in minutes may be best. If a student wants to complete a certain type of task with less help, then level of independence may be the right measure. If a student wants the quality of a skill to progress, the scale should describe the qualities of each step of progression.

To create a goal attainment scale, students and their teachers develop precise, leveled descriptions of progress. They begin by describing the starting point for the year on the skill in observable terms, and then determine and describe the end-of-year goal. Finally, students and their teachers pick intermediary points and describe these.

Note that goal attainment scales should be written in a way that allows measurement within the many authentic contexts of everyday classroom routines and activities. For example, the goal attainment scale in Figure 5.2, which is designed to measure progress in critical thinking on selecting and integrating information from credible sources, features nine increments of progress. Throughout the year, the student and teachers select the number that corresponds to the student's current performance, choosing the blank levels when the performance is between two points or increments.

Goal attainment scales can be used across the curriculum and in different daily contexts. Take a look back at Figure 5.1 and notice how Alyssa's progress was measured and mapped in four subject areas: language arts, social studies, art, and science. Keeping the data disaggregated by setting enables identifying whether a student is progressing more quickly in one setting than another, and whether a skill is being generalized across contexts.

Figure 5.2

SAMPLE GOAL ATTAINMENT SCALE

Critical Thinking: Analysis and Synthesis of Information		
Goal	9	Synthesizes information from multiple sources to make connections, highlight patterns in the information, draw conclusions, and reconcile any conflicting evidence or information.
	8	
Benchmark 3	7	Analyzes credible information from multiple sources to reveal similarities and differences in the evidence, information, and existing positions.
	6	
Benchmark 2	5	Uses multiple criteria for evaluating the credibility of information (e.g., authority of source, age of information, quality of the evidence, amount of evidence, convergence of information).
	4	
Benchmark 1	3	Uses 1–2 criteria for evaluating the credibility of information (e.g., authority of the source).
	2	
Baseline	1	Takes information from multiple sources and selects the information that is most relevant to the question being answered or position being taken.

Source Adapted from "Scales of Progress," by L. A. Jung, 2018b, *Educational Leadership, 75*(5), p. 24. Copyright 2018 ASCD.

With the individual student as well as potentially different teachers in different learning contexts all recording observations of the student's performance, it is essential that the scale uses simple, precise language, and that everyone understands the meaning of every level (Jung et al., 2008). Using goal attainment scaling, every teacher across all disciplines and settings can use the same scale to measure progress. Everyone concerned, including the student, is able understand and apply data to better inform instruction, support, and learning tactics.

Furthermore, goal attainment scaling offers the flexibility to use any type of measurement the team chooses, the means to collect and present data in the same way for all students and all goals, and an ability to measure in any context where the student has the opportunity to demonstrate the skill. The goal attainment scale and corresponding data map provide a broad-brush snapshot that allows teams to quickly determine progress.

The process of developing goal attainment scales with students also empowers students to become active in leading the development of their goals and measuring progress. What a wonderful opportunity to personalize learning and share ownership of the goal-setting and assessment process with students. By incorporating a goal attainment process within their daily activities, teachers can ensure that students with disabilities (and other students who need support) are blazing a trail that leads to their highest aspirations.

Explore Paths to the Dream

Students' IEPs are often devoid of guidance for what teachers will actually do to help students reach their goals. The popular IEP strategies of "verbal prompting, modeling, and praise" offer absolutely nothing of substance for teachers or students. Following the process of MAPs as we develop our IEPs leads to an actionable plan that includes concrete steps intended to support students as they work to meet their dreams.

The team needs to look at occupational as well as educational components of the desired outcomes to ensure alignment. Kelly's experience (see p. 103) provides one example. For another, consider a student who has expressed interest in becoming a veterinarian but does not want to attend college—an irreconcilable set of circumstances. The team's task now is to consider career paths that would allow that student to work with animals who are sick or in need of care but would *not* require years of postsecondary education. Becoming a vet tech might fit the bill perfectly. Or perhaps there are similar careers at an animal refuge or state park. Maybe there is a trade school that can support their aspirations. These conversations between a student and his or her team are not about "saying no" to a student's dream; they're about aligning occupational and educational goals to students' aspirations.

Ninth grader Valerie shared in her planning meeting that she wanted a career in pediatric nursing. When she was younger, she was diagnosed with leukemia, spent a lot of time in the hospital, and developed special relationships with the nurses. Valerie explained that she would like the opportunity to give back to kids undergoing similar experiences. Knowing this information, Valerie's team will be able to provide her with targeted occupational and educational experiences throughout the next four years of high school. This will give Valerie a better understanding of her long-term aspirations and how to pursue them after graduation.

When planning for one's future, there is seldom one clear-cut path. Most paths have their own challenges and limitations as the individual learns and grows. Educators need to empower students so that they can increase their *self-efficacy*—the belief that one is capable of completing something based on one's abilities. Students must have faith that the adults in their school are steering them toward the academic experiences and opportunities that will help them achieve their aspirations.

Leverage the Support of the Team

Each student comes to school every day with a unique blend of strengths and needs that defy easy pigeonholing. Information about students' families and previous school experiences can go a long way in helping general and special educators streamline and refine their efforts. Our colleague Barb Buswell, the executive director of the PEAK Parent Center in Colorado, likes to remind us that families are the keepers of their child's history. We will add to that by saying that educators who have previously taught the child are a rich information source as well. Yet too often we don't capitalize on the collective knowledge about a student with a disability, relying on the IEP to somehow capture this information. Over time, nuggets of insight can become lost inside an ever-expanding file of digital or paper forms. Teams end up spending the beginning of the school year trying to generate information about their students that was lost in the transition from one grade to the next.

To provide effective educational services to students, design meaningful lessons, accurately monitor student progress, and provide valuable input on IEPs, general educators need access to essential, relevant information about the students' academic and personal support needs. *Appreciative inquiry* is the practice of asking questions intended to unearth past successes in order to inform future actions. A student profile tool like the one in Figure 5.3 is a way to capture information regarding an individual student's needs and highlight how this information applies to a particular class. This kind of profile should be created jointly by family members, teachers, and others who are close to the student. It should reflect the decisions and strategies developed by the IEP team and address the following questions:

- **What are the specific IEP objectives addressed in this class?** These are taken from the IEP but are written in accessible language for teachers and families. Of course, the student is still accessing the *class* objectives, which come from the standards.
- **What are this student's areas of strength and interest?** This is an especially rich conversation to have with families, who have deep knowledge of what sustains their child's spirit. This type of information helps teachers when designing projects and class activities.
- **What aspirations does this student have?** Children and adolescents have educational and occupational aspirations. Knowledge of the student's personal aspirations, and the family's aspirations, can open up avenues for conversation and study.
- **What learning strategies and adaptations have been successful for this student?** This question is one that former teachers

Figure 5.3
STUDENT PROFILE TEMPLATE

Student name: Date: Profile completed by: Persons interviewed:
What are the specific IEP objectives addressed in the class?
What are this student's areas of strength and interest?
What aspirations does this student have?
What learning strategies and adaptations have been successful for this student?
Does this student use any informal or formal communication strategies? List them.
What positive behavioral support strategies seem to work for this student?
Does this student receive assessment accommodations? Describe them.
Is there other important family or health information that affects the education of this student?

can answer in detail—although they are rarely asked for input. Too often, what gets chronicled tends to be what *didn't* work. Past successful approaches provide clues for the student's new teachers regarding strategies they might try, too.

- **Does this student use any informal or formal communication strategies?** Some students may find it more comfortable to have a quick check-in before class starts or a wrap-up at the end. If the student uses augmentative or assistive communication supports, these should be included here.
- **What positive behavioral support strategies seem to work for this student?** Helpful hints about behavior supports (from family members or past teachers) are important and should be shared in a proactive way before they are needed.
- **Does this student receive assessment accommodations?** Some students require additional time on tests, oral versions of tests, or alternative forms. This should not be something that the teacher discovers for the first time on the eve of the first exam.
- **Is there other important family or health information that affects the education of this student?** Families often experience life-changing events that can shed light on student responses. The birth of a new baby or an elderly grandparent who has moved in can change family dynamics. Additional health information—a new glasses prescription, a broken wrist suffered last summer that hasn't completely healed, and so on—can be useful for teachers to know, too.

If you're thinking, *There's no one person who would know all this stuff,* that is exactly the point. The person who *oversees* the coordination and development of the student profile for students with IEPs may be the special education teacher, a case manager, or an assistant principal or department head, but *gathering this information is a group effort.* The special educators at the school where three of us work fill out student profiles during the home visits they pay to families of new incoming students with IEPs. Julie, as the special education director, adds pertinent information from the IEP. The general education teacher from the previous year is asked about successful approaches that should be continued. The net effect is that teams begin to share information that can fuel collaboration.

As with sharing ownership of goals with students, this process also needs to include the student's voice. The involvement of students in ways that are developmentally appropriate assists teams in ensuring that the opportunity to learn is properly aligned with expectations and aspirations. It also disrupts inadvertent tracking and ability grouping as teams brainstorm the various ways that students can be successful in general education classes. Instead of assuming that the student belongs in the lowest-level class or group, the team should focus on what it will take for the student to be successful anywhere. Student voice helps to fine-tune and calibrate expectations for the child.

Supporting the Evolution of Aspirations

Students need numerous opportunities to explore, research, experience, and reflect on their aspirations in order to refine them—or change them altogether. Lee Ann's husband, Chris, is a geologist; he was drawn to the field because of a love of the outdoors. What no one told Chris during his entire time in college was that, although geologists spend a lifetime studying elements of the Earth, most jobs in geology involve sitting at a desk indoors. Earlier exploration of the everyday requirements of actually being a geologist might have led Chris down a different path.

Christy is a 9th grader who has said she wants to be a doctor; she looks up to a family friend who is a pediatrician. However, instead of taking Christy's aspiration at face value and simply pointing her toward a pre-med course of study, her teachers engaged her in a conversation about the path to becoming a doctor. They learned that Christy wasn't keen on spending a lot of years in undergraduate and postgraduate work. They also learned that Christy prefers working on her own to interacting with people for extended periods. Next, they arranged for Christy to spend time shadowing a physician to get a clearer sense of what the career is like on a day-to-day basis. The result? Christy decided that being a physician didn't really align with how she wanted to live her life. However, she was still interested in medicine—a field with many careers requiring only a two- or four-year degree and involving less-frequent social interaction. Christy began refining her plan by exploring these other careers. If her teachers hadn't given her opportunities to explore and research these components, she would probably have continued down a path that ultimately would not have led to her happiness.

Starting Transition Planning Early

According to federal law and regulations, annual IEPs must include long-term transition goals *beginning at age 16* (IDEA, 2006). At 16, students are well into high school; frankly, this is too late to *begin* planning for life after high school, whether or not a student has a disability. Current practice generally involves establishing IEP goals year after year without having any conversations about a student's postschool goals and dreams—until basically right before they graduate or age out of services at age 22. An effective transition to adulthood requires years of planning, with benchmarks along the way to gauge progress toward the ultimate goal. Aspirational planning should be part of *every goal* developed in the IEP, not just the transition plan. Discussion and exploration must begin at an early age—in elementary school—to put into place the framework of supports, interventions, and coursework that support the student's goals.

Julie's 5-year-old nephew, Russell, wants to be an archeologist when he grows up; this has been Russell's dream since he was 3. He loves fossils and discovering new life from years before. Julie's 2-year-old nephew,

Daxton, wants to be a penguin. One of these dreams is possible; the other is not. However, instead of just telling Daxton that being a penguin is not realistic, his teachers and family wonder what it is about penguins that intrigues him. Does he want to live or work somewhere cold? Does he want to work *with* penguins? Or is there some other reason, imaginable to no one but Daxton himself?

Asking the right questions to shed light on the student's aspirations without stifling the student's dream can be challenging, but this is extremely important to the dreamer. With a shared understanding of what is driving students' dreams, the team can mobilize resources and opportunities to allow them to further explore and understand their aspirations.

Megan Knight, a 6th grade teacher, provided opportunities for her students to explore their career aspirations. She used this information to align readings, assessments, and experiences to support their exploration of these careers. She invited professionals into the classroom to speak about the different fields that aligned with her students' aspirations and planned field studies that supported this exploration. Because Ms. Knight knew her students and who they wanted to become, she was able to establish more relevance for them. She was also able to bring this knowledge into IEP meetings, to ensure that her students' goals aligned with their aspirations.

Clearly, the process of transition planning should happen for *every* student, not only students with identified disabilities. Just as disability status is irrelevant when delivering everyday instruction, it is irrelevant to transition planning, too. All students need assistance, experiences, and opportunities to explore and research their aspirations, and they need this early in their lives. Students with and without identified disabilities need our caring and intentional guidance on how to maneuver toward their educational and occupational aspirations. When we provide this guidance, we help to ensure that the instruction we deliver is equitable and focused on the whole child.

Conclusion

Investment in students' aspirations is the ultimate expression of equity-driven schooling. It communicates to students, "We see you." It signals to families, "We are here for you."

Unfortunately, expectations for students with IEPs can be undermined by inherent inequities that have persisted over time, the result of institutional blindness. Comments like "That's how we've always done it" or *"They* told us that this is the procedure we should follow" or *"They* said this is the best choice for those kids" basically send the message "I just work here"—distancing the speaker from any direct responsibility. Policies and procedures that are inherently unjust and inequitable are sustained by people who are "just doing their jobs." As Paulo Freire (1985) said, "Washing one's hands of the conflict between the powerful and the powerless means to side with the powerful, not to be neutral" (p. 122).

Where do you stand?

Changing the Approach to Student Aspirations

THE CHALLENGES	THE SOLUTIONS
Not all students within a school have access to all educational and extracurricular activities and opportunities.	Conduct an equity audit to identify gaps in opportunities and services. Create a school improvement design team that reflects diversity of thought, ability, and experience to analyze the data and develop an action plan addressing changes in processes and procedures.
Although well intentioned, teachers tend to be dream crushers—too ready to encourage students and families to think smaller and "face reality."	Train all members of the education team to function as dream managers, not dream crushers.
Students' IEP goals are limited to a single calendar year, focus on the immediate needs of students in particular environments, and do not address generalization or encourage students and their families to dream big.	Treat IEPs as living documents that require revisions as contexts, courses, dreams, and needs change. Use person-centered planning to develop action plans to help students pursue and achieve their dreams.
Transition plans are required and developed only for students with IEPs, and only after these students turn 16.	Begin transition planning for all students when they enter the school system. Treat aspirational planning as part of the general curriculum, aligning learning with individual aspirations. Document and track transition planning along with quarterly grades.
IEPs are drafted and almost complete before families and students are invited to contribute.	Use student profiles, developed annually in partnership with families, to capture successes, continuing challenges, and other relevant information.
IEPs do not provide sufficient detail and a progression of goal attainment that educators and students can use on a daily basis.	Use goal attainment scales provide teachers and students with reliable ways to measure progress.

Download this graphic at www.ascd.org/ASCD/pdf/books/jung2019.pdf

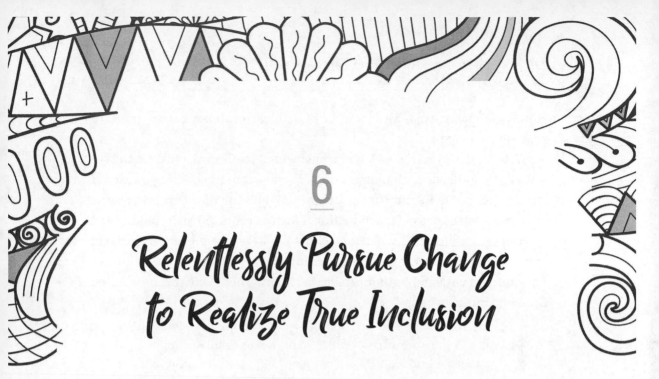

6

Relentlessly Pursue Change to Realize True Inclusion

"If you build it, they will come."

We quoted the film *Field of Dreams* in Chapter 2 as a warning about the inevitability of filling segregated classrooms and schools when those facilities exist. As long as there are segregated classrooms, programs, and schools, there will be students who "need" them. But we believe that there is a hopeful interpretation, too: build an equitable and inclusive education system in your school or district, and you will see students and educators rising to new levels of excellence.

Clark Elementary School took its first steps toward an inclusive service delivery system when it closed its segregated classrooms (Fisher, Sax, & Grove, 2000) and partnered with the local university for technical assistance and action planning. Neighborhood students with significant disabilities, previously educated in "cluster programs" elsewhere in the city, were invited back.

At the beginning of the new school year, some special education teachers and paraprofessionals at Clark were identified as full-time inclusion support providers. One special educator–paraprofessional team worked in upper-grade classrooms, while the other team worked in primary classrooms. Students with disabilities were dispersed throughout the general education classrooms. Members of the education team collaborated to share areas of expertise.

Within three years, Clark had transformed itself into a fully inclusive school. Despite some challenges outside the school's control—a teacher strike, a decrease in enrollment due to the opening of a new school, the sudden statewide class-size reduction plan that required hiring additional teachers—the vision of what the school could become carried through, and a system for ongoing communication about education opportunities for students with and without IEPs was maintained. One teacher shared this reflection:

> I know teachers will say, "Oh no, I don't think inclusion will work." I think we all dealt with "Oh no, not one more thing, one more person added to the classroom." But when we set up the program, we met as a committee, and we had a clear idea of what we wanted for the children. We had a very supportive administration and an excellent resource teacher. We worked on the model, went to the staff and got their ideas, came back and worked on it, and met every couple of months. (Fisher et al., 2000, p. 221)

Nearly 20 years later, Clark Elementary continues to operate under the tenets of true inclusion. Collaboration among faculty has been a key to their success, along with a deeply ingrained set of values about equity in education and the importance of honoring the individuality of each student. The most important takeaway from this school's journey is that an inclusive education system is not created through a single action but through many ongoing ones. The key to sustaining the work is a commitment to enact positive change. The only way to conclude this book is to look a little closer at what this commitment entails.

Building Social Capital

In an effort to close the achievement gaps among various targeted groups of students, schools often look for new interventions and curricula while overlooking the power of social capital. *Social capital* describes the norms, relationships, collegiality, and level of trust within an organization. The members of a school (an organization) include not only the paid professionals who work there but also its students, their families, and the surrounding community. To put it another way, a school organization with high social capital has all its oars in the water, rowing in synchronicity.

High organizational social capital is predictive of improved achievement scores for students in reading and mathematics and higher graduation rates. Further, schools with high organizational capital ameliorate other demographic school factors such as socioeconomic status, school size, and urbanicity (Salloum, Goddard, & Larsen, 2017). Conversely, when school organizations are divided into camps that must compete for scarce resources, social capital falls. And that is too often the case with special education; it's an isolated entity standing apart from the rest of the school.

Break Down Institutional Barriers

The National Equity Project advocates taking a *liberatory design* approach to facilitate innovation in K–12 schools and break down institutional barriers that perpetuate experiences where "students take separate journeys through the same school" (U.S. Department of Education Office for Civil Rights, 2016). Three assumptions underpin liberatory design:

- Design and decision-making processes predictably default to reproductive patterns.
- Design processes must create conditions for liberatory thinking and must be explicit about how oppression and power imbalances shape the design context within institutions.
- Design processes represent opportunities for decision makers to transform their own understanding of why persistent patterns of inequity exist in their context—and to transform their own relationships with those they are designing for. (National Equity Project, n.d., ¶ 3)

Liberatory design requires collaboration and partnership with those who will use and benefit from the system. It disrupts the notion that the designers (e.g., policymakers, administrators, other professionals) are the experts and, therefore, know best.

Frankly, it was allowing the "experts" to create the system that led to the problems we are now experiencing. In order for true innovation to take place, the design process must involve individuals with a variety of skills and perspectives, so that teams can build upon the strengths and experiences of others. Students with and without IEPs and their families need to be integral when redesigning the education system. This is how we build the organizational social capital of the school, and this is how we change the trajectory of achievement for all students.

Conduct an Equity Audit to Highlight Areas for Change

An equity audit focused on the opportunities that students have to learn can expose curricular inequities that might exist just below the surface, causing students to take separate journeys through the same school. Preparing for an equity audit requires planning and transparency, with transparency being the paramount concern. Audits should not be conducted until there is clarity on the purpose of the audit and its objectives and an agreement to act upon the results. Nothing is more discouraging than gathering and analyzing data and then having the findings shelved. Before an equity audit is conducted, the group charged with doing the work should discuss and reach consensus on the following questions (Soria & Ginsberg, 2016):

1. What do we want to learn from this process?
2. What is our focus?
3. How and to whom will we introduce and explain the opportunity?
4. How will we initially prioritize items or work with others to prioritize items?
5. Who will assist with the audit?
6. What is our timeline for introducing the audit, prioritizing items, collecting data, and generating results?

Equity audits can reveal uncomfortable truths about schools and the perceptions of students, teachers, families, and community members. A lack of commitment to act upon the results can lead to even more damage, as stakeholders realize that the organization lacks the courage to confront hard truths. But change never occurs without challenges; otherwise, everyone would do it.

Figure 6.1 presents some basic equity audit questions drawn from the collection in Smith, Frey, Pumpian, and Fisher's *Building Equity* (2017); it includes a simple rating scale to support self-assessment.

We encourage you to think of an equity audit as a tool for generating a big-picture view of experiences and perceptions. There is tremendous value in examining this information, because it shines a light on systems that need to change. But the issue of equitable education is also an individual one. The experiences of a child with a disability or an individual family speak just as loudly. The IEP process is the cornerstone of special education. Located at the intersection of policy, procedure, and practice, it's an essential means of making schooling more equitable for students with disabilities.

Establishing Mechanisms to Support Inclusion

Throughout the United States, students with IEPs and students of color are overrepresented in exclusionary disciplinary actions, including suspension and expulsion. In some U.S. schools, more than 25 percent of students with IEPs are suspended at least once per year (U.S. Department of Education Office of Special Education Programs, 2016). In some states, an African American student with a disability has a risk of suspension that is exponentially higher than the norm. In the 2013–14 school year, 21 percent of multiracial girls with IEPs faced out-of-school suspension for one or more days, compared with just 5 percent of white girls with IEPs (U.S. Department of Education Office for Civil Rights, 2016).

Figure 6.1
SAMPLE EQUITY AUDIT QUESTIONNAIRE

In our school...	Always True	Sometimes True	Never True
1. All students have the same access to class placement and course offerings.			
2. All students are encouraged to take challenging classes and undertake challenging assignments.			
3. Teachers of core classes know how to implement interventions to help all students succeed.			
4. We do not use tracking to group or schedule students.			
5. Teachers pay attention to students' abilities and challenges and are well prepared to differentiate instruction.			
6. All teachers are able to meet the needs of a diverse group of students.			
7. All teachers have high expectations for all students.			
8. Students know their teachers believe in them and that they are capable of challenging work.			
9. Students with disabilities have access to the full range of extracurricular clubs, projects, activities, and experiences.			

The school where Nancy, Doug, and Julie work opened as an inclusive school in 2007; from day one, students with IEPs have been educated alongside students without IEPs in the general education classroom. When it became apparent that the school had many of the same disproportionate suspension rates as other schools across the country, the staff committed to restorative practices (RP). This commitment has led to a significant reduction in suspension rates for students with and without IEPs.

The school's staff definitely made mistakes along the way—not with kids, but with one another. A particularly critical error was concentrating RP expertise in too few hands and not establishing proper communication. The school initially identified an administrator and a few interested educators to take on the lion's share of the RP work. For example, if a student got into a dust-up with a peer, the two were sequestered separately with RP Team members who used their training to prompt reflection, make amends, and fashion agreements. In many cases, these restorative efforts made out-of-school suspension unnecessary.

Sounds good, right? But consider what this looked like from the viewpoint of the classroom teacher. There was a conflict, the students in the conflict were removed, and later that period or the next day, these students were back in class. Adults who had witnessed the initial event had no idea what had happened in the meantime. They didn't know about the transformative discussions that had taken place, that the perpetrator had taken ownership of her actions, or that the victim had accepted the amends. They didn't know that regular follow-up meetings had been scheduled or that the parents, the counselor, and the student mentors were on board. All the classroom teacher knew was that something that seemed like an offense worthy of a suspension didn't result in a suspension, and now the students were back. In the minds of many teachers, restorative practices meant that "nothing happened."

Although students were transforming as members of the school community, the adults had failed to close the loop with the other adults, which put this innovative approach at risk of failing. In response, the RP Team designed a re-entry protocol that included not only follow-up plans for the students but also mechanisms for communication with teachers. Today, these re-entry plans are sent to the adults involved in any incident so that they are aware of what occurred, what will happen next, and where they can get more details and questions answered. The protocol includes the following information:

- A description of the incident and the parties involved (including the names of supporters for the offender and the victim, if they were part of the restorative conference)
- Commitments and consequences related to the incident
- Follow-up frequency, duration, and persons responsible (Smith, Fisher, & Frey, 2015).

We share this story to underscore how even a well-intentioned support mechanism can sabotage the best change efforts. Inclusive schools thrive on communication, and they must establish, monitor, and clarify the mechanisms that enable it. Creating inclusive education requires maintenance, monitoring, and a willingness to engage responsively with colleagues to continuously improve. Like the restorative practices work at Nancy, Doug, and Julie's school, the work to achieve equity and true inclusion is ongoing, never "done." It requires systematic, ongoing attention and support.

Changing the Paradigm

The whole idea of basing instructional decisions on disability status is rooted in a false dichotomy: an assumption that there is something different about students who qualify for an IEP. Sure, many students with disabilities need modified instruction, accommodations, and an individualized plan for growth. But many students who *don't* qualify for special education services also need these supports. As we discussed in Chapter 1, it isn't disability status that demands this individualization; it is a student's needs.

Ignoring the false dichotomy of disability unnecessarily pathologizes the needs of students who have IEPs and leads to some students (primarily students of color) being improperly labeled as having a disability. At the same time, this false dichotomy leads educators to neglect real needs of students who do not meet special education eligibility requirements, boxing them out from receiving the individualized services, or at least the accommodations, that would help them thrive. Changing the inclusion paradigm means providing quality instruction and supports to *all students*, IEP or no IEP. It also means setting challenging expectations for all students and designing and delivering the necessary supports so that all students can reach their goals. This work is more complex than any step-by-step process can fully capture, but we can offer the following high-level guidance, based on experience.

Set a Foundation by Changing the Culture

Before doing anything else, you need get a sense of the current climate. Figure 6.2 is a survey tool that can be used to gauge learning beliefs in your school and highlight areas on which you will need to focus when changing the culture.

Focus on Systemic Change

The least restrictive environment (LRE) is more than a box checked and completed on an IEP form. It is a student right and a moral imperative that every educator in the building must take very seriously. Rather than clustering students with disabilities in resource rooms or designated "inclusion classrooms" (thus risking both less effective instruction and teacher burnout), maximize inclusion by designing individualized supports for general education settings.

Realizing the spirit of LRE also requires reexamining service delivery models. Do you default to specialists providing direct support when a consultative approach could be as effective? Allowing special educators and specialists to coach general education teachers in the use of strategies that were once "reserved" for special education maximizes everyone's expertise. Creative strategies, such as using the infused skills grid and combining models of co-teaching with flexible grouping of students, will help you realize a more inclusive service delivery system.

As we have stressed through this book, inclusion is, at its core, an equity issue. Changing the paradigm has greater effects than providing a more

Figure 6.2
LEARNING BELIEFS SURVEY

Please respond to the following statements according to the scale below:

1 = Strongly Agree
2 = Agree Somewhat
3 = Disagree Somewhat
4 = Strongly Disagree

_____   1. I feel that our educational system is working.

_____   2. I feel that I have the training to implement high-quality instruction successfully.

_____   3. I feel that I cover less of the curriculum because of the focus on remediation.

_____   4. I feel that I have the time to implement quality instruction effectively.

_____   5. I feel that grades are fixed and should not be changed once assigned.

_____   6. I feel that it is difficult to modify instruction and my teaching style to meet the needs of all of my students.

_____   7. I feel that allowing students multiple opportunities to demonstrate mastery is fair.

_____   8. I feel that having other adults in my classroom is a problem.

_____   9. I feel that the behaviors of some students distract the rest of a class and take away from time spent teaching.

_____ 10. I feel that students take advantage of grading systems designed to be flexible.

Please complete this thought:

Learning is best accomplished when . . .

Source: From *How to Create a Culture of Achievement in Your School and Classroom* (p. 191), by D. Fisher, N. Frey, and I. Pumpian, 2012, Alexandria, VA: ASCD. Copyright 2012 by ASCD.

effective education with better outcomes for students, although this in itself is enough of a rationale to do so. The fact is, all students *deserve* the opportunity to receive the best instruction possible, within the general education classroom, from a general education teacher, alongside their peers. Separate is not equal, and this applies to administrative structures. A seamless education and service delivery system not only complies with the letter and spirit of the Individuals with Disabilities Education Act, it also has the potential to serve more students, to provide improved services, and to realize better outcomes.

In this model of student support, the building principal supervises and coaches the entire education team—special education and general education staff. Planning time, in-service training, and grade-level or department meetings should include all instructional staff. Realizing the spirit of inclusion requires much more than meeting the letter of the law and placing students with disabilities in regular classrooms. In other words, it's about more than where services will be delivered. It's a belief or philosophy from which educators operate. A team-based model of student support means that every decision is a team decision—from which students need support to who designs intervention and how that intervention is implemented. The goal is ensuring all students can access and learn the general curriculum.

Develop an Action Plan to Implement the Team-Based Model

Implementing a team-based model of student support is a complex undertaking, different from what most educators were prepared for during their teacher education programs (i.e., the "expert approach"; see Figure 6.3). Transitioning to such a model will require investment in the ongoing professional learning of every adult on campus, both certificated and classified. Paraprofessionals deserve to improve their craft to support all students, including those who have IEPs. Co-teaching teams benefit from training that allows them to strengthen their instructional responsiveness. Invest in collaborative practices that build trust among faculty.

Figure 6.3

EXPERT VS. TEAM-BASED MODELS OF STUDENT SUPPORT

Decision	Expert Approach	Team-Based Approach
Eligibility for support	Support is provided when students demonstrate eligibility for special education services.	Support is provided to any student who is significantly below grade level on critical general curriculum skills, regardless of the presence of a diagnosis.
Goal development	Goals focus mostly on performance on developmental or standardized test and performance in special education settings.	Goals focus on student mastery of standards in the general education curriculum and mastery of needs-based IEP objectives, including the routines of the school day.
Design of support	The expert/specialist designs intervention based on student needs.	The team designs support based on student needs and the context of the general curriculum.
Delivery of support	The expert/specialist implements support.	A team implements support.
Location of support	Most students spend the majority of their day in general education classrooms, but individualized goals are supported outside the general education classroom.	Students' individualized goals are supported with instruction and intervention in the general education classroom to the greatest extent possible. Goals are only supported outside the general education classroom if they cannot be achieved there.
Relation of support to the general curriculum	Students are often removed from the general education setting and provided with *replacement* instruction.	Almost all students remain in the general education classroom for instruction and receive *supplemental* instruction.

Asking them to engage in role release requires a great deal of trust in colleagues, in the school leader, and in the organization.

To implement this new model of inclusion in your school, you will need to develop an action plan. Figure 6.4 is a tool that has been adapted and modified over the years, and it has been implemented in school systems around the world. In fact, we have used this tool in our own schools with great success.

Notice that Step 1 of this model is to review the strengths of your education team in the areas of curriculum, instruction, professional development, organizational design, and collaboration. For example, maybe your school's strength is the collaborative work teachers have done to align the curriculum vertically and horizontally to reduce gaps and redundancies. Or maybe your school provides strong professional learning for all instructional staff, meaning that all teachers have access to information, the coaching that will help them implement what they learn, and a series of reflective cycles to determine the effect of their efforts.

This review of strengths will naturally lead, in Step 2, to identifying the possibilities this new vision of inclusion presents to your school and its stakeholders and also the challenges you may have to face to implement it. Consider again the areas of curriculum, instruction, professional development, organizational design, and collaboration. Maybe your school's progress will be delayed by the varied quality of instruction that students receive from different teachers who teach the same grade or content. Maybe teachers in your school lack collaboration time and the will to communicate about specific students' needs. The latter is sometimes attributable to teachers worrying that they are going to be judged or feeling that asking for help is as sign of weakness.

Establishing your school's vision of inclusion also requires negotiating and discussing goals—and what it takes to achieve them. In Step 3, your action team will need to focus on what your school would look like if you were able to realize the dream. Consider the look, feel, and sound of the school as perceived by students, families, teachers, site leaders, district

Figure 6.4
ACTION PLAN TEMPLATE FOR TRANSITIONING TO INCLUSIVE PRACTICES

District: Date:

Leadership Team:

Members:

Step 1: Identify Data-Based Strengths: Current Level of Inclusive Practices

System Component	What are our **strengths**?	What can we **build upon**?
Curriculum		
Instruction		
Professional Development		
Organizational Design		
Collaboration/Communication Between Special Education and General Education		

Step 2: Consider Data-Based Implications: Possibilities and Challenges of Inclusion

System Component	What are the **possibilities**?	What are the **challenges**?
Curriculum		
Instruction		
Professional Development		
Organizational Design		
Collaboration/Communication Between Special Education and General Education		

Step 3: Create a Vision for the Transition: Desired State for Inclusive Practices

Describe/illustrate successful implementation of inclusion across your system and among your stakeholders.

Stakeholder Group	What does inclusion **look** like?	What does inclusion **sound** like?	What does inclusion **feel** like?
Students			
Families			
Teachers			
School Leaders			
District Leaders			
Community Members			
Partners and Providers			

(continued)

Figure 6.4
ACTION PLAN TEMPLATE FOR TRANSITIONING
TO INCLUSIVE PRACTICES *(continued)*

Step 4: Data-Based Planning: The Move from the Current State to the Desired State

Fill out a copy of this planning sheet for each of your goals.

Goal Name:	
Action Steps What are the necessary steps to successfully accomplish the goal?	
Leadership and Partners Who is responsible for moving the goal forward and who will support efforts? Consider —Point person —Shared leadership —Collaborative partners	
Resources What resources are needed? Consider —People —Time —Materials —Funding	

Success Indicators	
How will we know when we are successful? Include —Criteria —Method —Evidence	
Time Line	
When will the work occur? Indicate —Range from beginning to end Milestone What are the deadlines? —Completion Date —Evaluation	

Source: "Colorado Standards Transition Plan Template," in *Transition Action Planning Guide—DRAFT* (12–19), by the Colorado Department of Education, 2012. Copyright 2012 by the Colorado Department of Education. Adapted with permission.

leaders, community members, and partners or providers. For example, do you want to *hear* students supporting one another? Do you want to *see* interaction between students with and without IEPs in noninstructional environments as well as in class?

Step 4 is about mapping the specific action steps that will help you achieve each goal of your desired state: identifying leadership activities, partnerships, resources, and success indicators—and establishing a timeline.

As an illustration, consider the goal of closing special education self-contained classrooms and integrating the students into general education settings in natural proportions with appropriate support provided by general and special educators. Action steps might include talking with families, providing professional learning opportunities for teachers, reviewing IEPs and scheduling midyear meetings as necessary, identifying peer supports, and reevaluating the master schedule. Leadership activities might involve the principal sharing the plan with district leadership and attending midyear IEP meetings. For resources, the school might allocate funds for planning time and release time for teams to visit other successful schools. Success indicators could be the completion of the midyear IEPs, the first day of participation in general education classes for students with IEPs, and the first grade-report period with a high percentage of students succeeding. The timeline might require three months to ensure that all of this work has been completed.

Making plans is one thing; implementation is another. Monitoring the plan is crucial to its success. Students with and without IEPs deserve more than their teachers and school leaders simply *attempting* implementation. They deserve a system of support that focuses on the seamless inclusion of students with IEPs in all settings, challenge and support for all students, progress monitoring of student learning, and rapid responses when changes are needed. They deserve for their teachers to have high expectations for their success.

Perhaps this is the keystone of inclusion: *expect that all students will succeed and commit to that belief.* Without high expectations, we can most certainly predict a grim outcome. Teacher expectations top Hattie's list of influences on students' learning (2012). Expect more, and you will get more. Teacher expectations become students' reality. And, while you're at it, make sure to expect more of yourself as well.

Conclusion

The actions outlined in this book are underpinned by a set of values and beliefs about the kind of schools that students deserve. We firmly believe that the widespread experience of inequitable schooling results from a host of institutional and sociocultural factors that require systemic change. While individual teachers might make changes to their own class-rooms, these efforts in and of themselves are not enough. And it's true that many students have been fortunate enough to encounter individuals who have had a positive influence and have altered the trajectory of their young lives in a positive way. But too many students, especially those with IEPs, have not benefited in the same way. Their aspirations are not inten-tionally and purposefully nurtured, and over time, they fall short of their potential—if their potential is ever even recognized.

We hope this book has stirred you and connected to your moral com-pass. Our call to action is for *every educator*. Every student belongs to all of us, and this realization is where we start. Change begins with the indi-vidual, but it doesn't end there. Talk about issues of inclusion and equity whenever you can. Make it known that this is something of primary importance in your professional life. You will be surprised at how quickly your allies will reveal themselves.

All STUDENTS are Our STUDENTS

A Culture of Equity and Inclusion

Structures That Honor the Spirit of LRE

Student Aspirations Valued and Pursued

All Educators Supporting All Students

Collaborative Instruction and Intervention

Undoing marginalization and changing expectations prepares our students to thrive in the world.

References

Arndt, K., & Liles, J. (2010). Preservice teachers' perceptions of coteaching: A qualitative study. *Action in Teacher Education, 32*(1), 15–25. doi:10.1080/01626620.2010.10463539

Baer, R. M., Flexer, R. W., Beck, S., Amstutz, N., Hoffman, L., Brothers, J., . . . Zechman, C. (2003). A collaborative followup study on transition service utilization and post-school outcomes. *Career Development for Exceptional Individuals, 26,* 7–25. doi:10.1177/088572880302600102

Boccio, D. E., Weisz, G., & Lefkowitz, R. (2016). Administrative pressure to practice unethically and burnout within the profession of school psychology. *Psychology in the Schools, 53,* 659–672. doi:10.1002/pits.21931

Bowman-Perrott, L., Davis, H., Vannest, K., Williams, L., Greenwood, C., & Parker, R. (2013). Academic benefits of peer tutoring: A meta-analytic review of single-case research. *School Psychology Review, 42*(1), 39–55.

Brock, M. E., & Huber, H. B. (2017). Are peer support arrangements an evidence-based practice? A systematic review. *Journal of Special Education, 51,* 150–163. doi:10.1177/0022466917708184

Brock, M. E., & Schaefer, J. M. (2015). Location matters: Geographic location and educational placement of students with developmental disabilities. *Research and Practice for Persons with Severe Disabilities, 40,* 154–164. doi:10.1177/1540796915591988

Burke, S. (2017, March). *Why design should include everyone* [Video file]. Retrieved from https://www.ted.com/talks/sinead_burke_why_design_should_include_everyone

Burns, M. K., Egan, A. M., Kunkel, A. K., McComas, J., Peterson, M. M., Rahn, N. L., & Wilson, J. (2013). Training for generalization and maintenance in RtI implementation: Front-loading for sustainability. *Learning Disabilities Research & Practice, 28*(2), 81–88.

Calabrese, R., Patterson, J., Liu, F., Goodvin, S., Hummel, C., & Nance, E. (2008). An appreciative inquiry into the Circle of Friends program: The benefits of social inclusion of students with disabilities. *International Journal of Whole Schooling, 4*(2), 20–48.

Carter, E. W., Moss, C. K., Hoffman, A., Chung, Y-C., & Sisko, L. (2011). Efficacy and social validity of peer support arrangements for adolescents with disabilities. *Exceptional Children, 78,* 107–125. doi:10.1177/001440291107800107

Carter, E., Sisco, L. G., Brown, L., & Brickham, D. (2008). Peer interactions and academic engagement of youth with developmental disabilities in inclusive middle and high school classrooms. *American Journal of Mental Retardation: AJMR, 113,* 479–494. doi:10.1352/2008.113:479-494

Castro-Villarreal, F., Rodriguez, B. J., & Moore, S. (2014). Teachers' perceptions and attitudes about Response to Intervention (RTI) in their schools: A qualitative analysis. *Teaching and Teacher Education, 40,* 104–112. doi:10.1016/j.tate.2014.02.004

Cole, C., Waldron, N., & Majd, M. (2004). Academic progress of students across inclusive and traditional settings. *Mental Retardation, 42,* 136–144. doi:10.1352/0047-6765(2004)42 <136:APOSAI>2.0.CO;2

Colorado Department of Education. (2012). *Transition action planning guide—DRAFT.* Retrieved from http://www.cde.state.co.us/standardsandinstruction/tapguide

Cooc, N., & Kiru, E. W. (2018). Disproportionality in special education: A synthesis of international research and trends. *Journal of Special Education, 52,* 163–173.

Cushing, L. S., & Kennedy, C. H. (1997). Academic effects of providing peer support in general education classrooms on students without disabilities. *Journal of Applied Behavior Analysis, 30,* 139–151. doi:10.1901/jaba.1997.30-139

Cytrynbaum, S., Ginath, Y., Birdwell, J., & Brandt, L. (1979). Goal attainment scaling: A critical review. *Evaluation Quarterly, 3,* 5–40. doi:10.1177/0193841X7900300102

Delpit, L. (2006). *Other people's children: Cultural conflict in the classroom.* New York: New Press.

Dumont, H., Protsch, P., Jansen, M., & Becker, M. (2017). Fish swimming into the ocean: How tracking relates to students' self-beliefs and school disengagement at the end of schooling. *Journal of Educational Psychology, 109,* 855–870. doi:10.1037/edu0000175

Dunn, M. E., Shelnut, J., Ryan, J. B., & Katsiyannis, A. (2017). A systematic review of peer-mediated interventions on the academic achievement of students with emotional/behavioral disorders. *Education & Treatment of Children, 40,* 497–524. doi:10.1353/etc.2017.0022

Embich, J. L. (2001). The relationship of secondary special education teachers' roles and factors that lead to professional burnout. *Teacher Education and Special Education, 24,* 58–69. doi:10.1177/088840640102400109

Etscheidt, S. K. (2006). Progress monitoring: Legal issues and recommendations for IEP teams. *TEACHING Exceptional Children, 38*(3), 56–60. doi:10.1177/004005990603800308

Feldman, R., Carter, E. W., Asmus, J., & Brock, M. E. (2016). Presence, proximity, and peer interactions of adolescents with severe disabilities in general education classrooms. *Exceptional Children, 82,* 192–208. doi:10.1177/0014402915585481

Fisher, D., & Frey, N. (2003). Writing instruction for struggling adolescent readers: A gradual release model. *Journal of Adolescent and Adult Literacy, 46,* 396–407.

Fisher, D., & Frey, N. (2010). *Enhancing RTI: How to ensure success with effective classroom instruction and intervention.* Alexandria, VA: ASCD.

Fisher, D., & Frey, N. (2011). *The purposeful classroom: How to structure lessons with learning goals in mind.* Alexandria, VA: ASCD.

Fisher, D., & Frey, N. (2014a). *Better learning through structured teaching: A framework for the gradual release of responsibility* (2nd ed.). Alexandria, VA: ASCD.

Fisher, D., & Frey, N. (2014b). What 20+ years of secondary inclusion has taught us. In S. Danforth (Ed.), *Becoming a great inclusive educator* (pp. 285–292). New York: Peter Lang.

Fisher, D., Frey, N., & Lapp, D. (2011). What the research says about intentional instruction. In S. J. Samuels & A. Farstrup (Eds.), *What the research has to say about reading instruction* (4th ed., pp. 359–378). Newark, DE: International Reading Association.

Fisher, D., Frey, N., & Pumpian, I. (2012). *How to create a culture of achievement in your school and classroom.* Alexandria, VA: ASCD.

Fisher, D., Roach, V., & Frey, N. (2002). Examining the general programmatic benefits on inclusive schools. *International Journal of Inclusive Education, 6*(1), 63–78.

Fisher, D., Sax, C., & Grove, K. (2000). The resilience of changes promoting inclusiveness in an urban elementary school. *Elementary School Journal, 100,* 213–227. doi:10.1086/499640

Fisher, D., Sax, C., & Pumpian, I. (1996). From intrusion to inclusion: Myths and realities in our schools. *The Reading Teacher, 49,* 580–584.

Fisher, D., Sax, C., Rodifer, K., & Pumpian, I. (1999). Teachers' perspectives of curriculum and climate changes: Benefits of inclusive education. *Journal for a Just and Caring Education, 5,* 256–268.

Fisher, K. W., & Shogren, K. A. (2016). The influence of academic tracking on adolescent social networks. *Remedial and Special Education, 37,* 89–100. doi:10.1177/0741932515616758

Fletcher, J. M., & Vaughn, S. (2009). Response to Intervention: Preventing and remediating academic difficulties. *Child Development Perspectives, 3*(1), 30–37. doi:10.1111/j.1750-8606.2008.00072.x

Flexer, R. W., Daviso, A. W., Baer, R. M., Queen, R. M., & Meindl, R. S. (2011). An epidemiological model of transition and postschool outcomes. *Career Development for Exceptional Individuals, 34,* 83–94. doi:10.1177/0885728810387922

Foreman, P., Arthur-Kelly, M., Pascoe, S., King, B. S., & Downing, J. (2004). Evaluating the educational experiences of students with profound and multiple disabilities in inclusive and segregated classroom settings: An Australian perspective. *Research and Practice for Persons with Severe Disabilities, 29,* 183–193. doi:10.2511/rpsd.29.3.183

Freedman, M. K. (2005). *Grades, report cards, etc. . . . and the law.* Boston: School Law Pro.

Freire, P. (1985). *The politics of education: Culture, power and liberation.* South Hadley, MA: Bergin & Garvey.

Friend, M., & Cook, L. (2007). *Interactions: Collaboration skills for school professionals* (5th ed.). Boston: Allyn & Bacon.

Fuchs, L. S., Fuchs, D., Hamlett, C. L., Hope, S. K., Hollenbeck, K. N., Capizzi, A. M., . . . Brothers, R. L. (2006). Extending responsiveness-to-intervention to math problem-solving at third grade. *TEACHING Exceptional Children, 38*(4), 59–63. doi:10.1177/004005990603800409

Gage, N. A., Whitford, D. K., & Katsiyannis, A. (2018). A review of schoolwide positive behavior interventions and supports as a framework for reducing disciplinary exclusions. *Journal of Special Education, 52,* 142–151. doi:10.1177/0022466918767847

Giangreco, M. F. (2010). One-to-one paraprofessionals for students with disabilities in inclusive classrooms: Is conventional wisdom wrong? *Intellectual and Developmental Disabilities, 48,* 1–13. doi:10.1352/1934-9556-48.1.1

Giangreco, M. F. (2013). Teacher assistant supports in inclusive schools: Research, practices, and alternatives. *Australian Journal of Special Education, 37*(2), 93–106.

Giangreco, M. F., & Doyle, M. B. (2015). Italy presses forward in educating students with learning disabilities. *Phi Delta Kappan, 97*(3), 23–28. doi:10.1177/0031721715614824

Giangreco, M. F., Yuan, S., McKenzie, B., Cameron, P., & Fialka, J. (2005). "Be careful what you wish for . . . ": Five reasons to be concerned about the assignment of individual paraprofessionals. *TEACHING Exceptional Children, 37*(5), 28–34. doi:10.1177/004005990503700504

Gordon, L. (Producer), Gordon, C. (Producer), & Robinson, P. A. (Director). (1989). *Field of dreams* [Motion picture]. United States: Universal Pictures.

Gorey, K. M. (2009). Comprehensive school reform: Meta-analytic evidence of black-white achievement gap narrowing. *Education Policy Analysis Archives, 17*(25), 1–14. doi:10.14507/epaa.v17n25.2009

Hampden-Thompson, G., Diehl, J., & Kinukawa, A. (2007). *Description and employment criteria of instructional paraprofessionals* (NCES 2007-008). Washington, DC: National Center for Educational Statistics. Retrieved from https://nces.ed.gov/pubs2007/2007008.pdf

Hattie, J. (2012). *Visible learning for teachers.* New York: Routledge.

Hattie, J., & Timperley, H. (2007). The power of feedback. *Review of Educational Research, 77,* 81–112. doi:10.3102/003465430298487

Hillesøy, S. (2016). The contribution of support teachers in facilitating children's peer interactions. *International Journal of Early Childhood, 48,* 95–109. doi:10.1007/s13158-016-0157-1

Individuals with Disabilities Education Act, 20 U.S.C. §§ 1400 et seq. (2006 & Supp. V. 2011).

Joshi, G. S., & Bouck, E. C. (2017, February). Examining postsecondary education predictors and participation for students with learning disabilities. *Journal of Learning Disabilities, 50*(1), 3–13. doi:10.1177/0022219415572894

Jung, L. A. (2017a, May 17). Differentiated assessment and grading model (DiAGraM) [Blog post]. Retrieved from https://www.leadinclusion.org/single-post/2017/05/17/Differentiated-Assessment-and-Grading-Model-DiAGraM

Jung, L. A. (2017b). In providing supports for students, language matters. *Educational Leadership, 74*(7), 42–45.

Jung, L. A. (2018a). *From goals to growth: Intervention and support in every classroom.* Alexandria, VA: ASCD.

Jung, L. A. (2018b). Scales of progress. *Educational Leadership, 75*(5), 22–27.

Jung, L. A., & Akers, K. S. (2016, February). *Equity in access to early intervention services.* Paper presented at the Biennial Conference on Research Innovations in Early Intervention, San Diego, CA.

Jung, L. A., Gomez, C., Baird, S. M., & Galyon Keramidas, C. L. (2008, September). Designing intervention plans: Bridging the gap between individualized education programs and implementation. *TEACHING Exceptional Children, 41*(1), 26–33. doi.org/10.1177/004005990804100103

Katz, J., Mirenda, P., & Auerbach, S. (2002). Instructional strategies and educational outcomes for students with developmental disabilities in inclusive "multiple intelligences" and typical inclusive classrooms. *Research and Practice for Persons with Severe Disabilities, 27,* 227–238. doi:10.2511/rpsd.27.4.227

Kirby, M. (2017). Implicit assumptions in special education policy: Promoting full inclusion for students with learning disabilities. *Child & Youth Care Forum, 46,* 175–191. doi:10.1007/s10566-016-9382-x

Kliewer, C., Biklen, D., & Kasa-Hendrickson, C. (2006). Who may be literate? Disability and resistance to the cultural denial of competence. *American Educational Research Journal, 43,* 163–192. doi:10.3102/00028312043002163

Kurth, J. A. (2015). Educational placement of students with autism: The impact of state of residence. *Focus on Autism and Other Developmental Disabilities, 30*(4), 249–256.

Lombardi, A., Doren, B., Gau, J. M., & Lindstrom, L. E. (2013). The influence of instructional settings in reading and math on postsecondary participation. *Journal of Disability Policy Studies, 24,* 170–180. doi:10.1177/1044207312468766

Manset, G., & Semmel, M. I. (1997). Are inclusive programs for students with mild disabilities effective? A comparative review of model programs. *Journal of Special Education, 31,* 155–180. doi:10.1177/002246699703100201

Morningstar, M., Kurth, J. A., & Johnson, P. E. (2017). Examining national trends in educational placements for students with significant disabilities. *Remedial & Special Education, 38,* 3–12. doi:10.1177/0741932516678327

Morrier, M. J., & Gallagher, P. A. (2010). Racial disparities in preschool special education eligibility for five southern states. *Journal of Special Education, 46,* 152–169. doi: 10.1177/0022466910380465

National Center for Education Statistics. (2017). *The digest of education statistics, 2016* (52nd ed.) (NCES 2017-094).Washington, DC: Institute of Education Sciences, U.S. Department of Education.

National Equity Project. (n.d.). *Liberatory design.* Retrieved from http://nationalequity project.org/services/liberatory-design

O'Brien, J., Pearpoint, J., & Kahn, L. (2010). *The PATH & MAPS handbook.* Toronto, ON: Inclusion Press.

Okilwa, N. S. A., & Shelby, L. (2010). The effects of peer tutoring on academic performance of students with disabilities in grades 6 through 12: A synthesis of the literature. *Remedial and Special Education, 31,* 450–463. doi:10.1177/0741932509355991

Pearson, P. D., & Gallagher, M. C. (1983). The instruction of reading comprehension. *Contemporary Educational Psychology, 8,* 317–344. doi:10.1016/0361- 476X(83)90019-X

Raspa, M., Hebbeler, K., Bailey, D. R., & Scarborough, A. A. (2010). Service provider combinations and the delivery of early intervention services to children and families. *Infants & Young Children, 23,* 132–144. doi:10.1097/IYC.0b013e3181d230f9

Rea, P. J., McLaughlin, V. L., & Walther-Thomas, C. (2002). Outcomes for students with learning disabilities in inclusive and pullout programs. *Exceptional Children, 68,* 203–223. doi:10.1177/001440290206800204

Reardon, S. F., Grewal, E., Kalogrides, D., & Greenberg, E. (2012). *Brown* fades: The end of court-ordered desegregation and the resegregation of American public schools. *Journal of Policy Analysis and Management, 31,* 876–904. doi:10.1002/pam.21649

Rojewski, J. W., Lee, I. H., & Gregg, N. (2013). Causal effects of inclusion on postsecondary education outcomes of individuals with high-incidence disabilities. *Journal of Disability Policy Studies, 25,* 210–219. doi:10.1177/1044207313505648

Ruble, L. A., McGrew, J., Dalrymple, N., & Jung, L. A. (2010). Examining the quality of IEPs for young children with autism. *Journal of Autism and Developmental Disorders, 40,* 1459–1470. doi:10.1007/s10803-010-1003-1

Ruble, L. A., McGrew, J. H., Toland, M. D., Dalrymple, N. J., & Jung, L. A. (2013). A randomized controlled trial of COMPASS web-based and face-to-face teacher coaching in autism. *Journal of Consulting and Clinical Psychology, 81,* 566–572. doi:10.1037/a0032003

Salloum, S., Goddard, R., & Larsen, R. (2017). Social capital in schools: A conceptual and empirical analysis of the equity of its distribution and relation to academic achievement. *Teachers College Record, 119*(7), 1–29.

SAP. (2013). Autism at work [Video file]. Retrieved from https://www.sap.com/corporate/en/company/diversity/differently-abled.html

Scruggs, T. E., & Mastropieri, M. A. (2017). Making inclusion work with co-teaching. *TEACHING Exceptional Children, 49,* 284–293. doi:10.1177/0040059916685065

Shifrer, D. (2013). Stigma of a label: Educational expectations for high school students labeled with learning disabilities. *Journal of Health and Social Behavior, 54,* 462–480. doi:10.1177/0022146513503346

Smith, D., Fisher, D., & Frey, N. (2015). *Better than carrots or sticks: Restorative practices for positive classroom management.* Alexandria, VA: ASCD.

Smith, D., Frey, N., Pumpian, I., & Fisher, D. (2017). *Building equity: Policies and practices to empower all learners.* Alexandria, VA: ASCD.

Snow, K. (2005). To ensure inclusion, freedom, and respect for all we must use people first language. Retrieved from https://www.cde.state.co.us/sites/default/files/documents/early/downloads/prespedonlinecourses/peoplefirst.pdf

Soria, L., & Ginsberg, M. (2016). Questions that lead to action. *Journal of Staff Development, 37*(5), 28–35.

Soukup, J. H., Wehmeyer, M. L., Bashinski, S. M., & Bovaird, J. (2007). Classroom variables and access to the general curriculum for students with disabilities. *Exceptional Children, 74,* 101–120. doi:10.1177/001440290707400106

Stormont, M. S., Reinke, W., & Herman, K. (2011). Teachers' knowledge of evidence-based interventions and available school resources for children with emotional and behavioral problems. *Journal of Behavioral Education, 20,* 138–147. doi:10.1007/s10864-011-9122-0

Szumski, G., Smogorzewska, J., & Karwowski, M. (2017). Academic achievement of students without special educational needs in inclusive classrooms: A meta-analysis. *Educational Research Review, 21,* 33–54. doi:10.1016/j.edurev.2017.02.004

Torgesen, J. K. (2002). The prevention of reading difficulties. *Journal of School Psychology, 40,* 7–26. doi:10.1016/S0022-4405(01)00092-9

United Nations General Assembly. (2007, January 24). *Resolution adopted by the General Assembly on 13 December 2006. Convention on the rights of persons with disabilities.* Retrieved from http://www.un.org/ga/search/view_doc.asp?symbol=A/RES/61/106

U.S. Department of Education Office for Civil Rights. (2016). *2013–14 civil rights action data collection: A first look: Key data highlights on equity and opportunity gaps in our nation's public schools.* Retrieved from https://www2.ed.gov/about/offices/list/ocr/docs/2013-14-first-look.pdf

U. S. Department of Office of Special Education Programs. (2016, February). *Racial and ethnic disparities in special education: A multi-year disproportionality analysis by state, analysis category, and race/ethnicity.* Washington, DC: Author.

U.S. Government Accountability Office [GAO]. (2016, April). *K–12 education: Better use of information could help agencies identify disparities and address racial discrimination* (GAO-16-345). Washington, DC: Author. Retrieved from https://www.gao.gov/products/GAO-16-345

Villa, R. A., & Thousand, J. S. (2016). *Leading an inclusive school: Access and success for ALL students.* Alexandria, VA: ASCD.

Wagner, M., Newman, L., Cameto, R., Levine, P., & Marder, C. (2003). *Going to school: Instructional contexts, programs, and participation of secondary school students with disabilities. A report from the National Longitudinal Transition Study-2 (NLTS2).* Menlo Park, CA: SRI International.

Westling, D. L., & Fox, L. (2009). *Teaching students with severe disabilities* (4th ed.). Upper Saddle River, NJ: Merrill.

Wong, K. K., & Meyer, S. J. (1998). Title I schoolwide programs: A synthesis of findings from recent evaluation. *Educational Evaluation and Policy Analysis, 20,* 115–136. doi:10.3102/01623737020002115

Index

The letter *f* following a page locator denotes a figure.

About the Authors

Lee Ann Jung is the founder of Lead Inclusion, a clinical professor at San Diego State University, and a consultant to schools worldwide. She provides support to schools in the areas of inclusion, standards-based learning and grading, designing individualized goals and interdisciplinary supports, and measuring progress. Before entering higher education, Jung worked in the roles of special education teacher and administrator in Alabama. Although her background is special education, she no longer considers herself a special educator; she is an inclusive educator. Jung has written numerous publications in the areas of inclusion and assessment and is the author of the ASCD book *From Goals to Growth: Intervention and Support in Every Classroom*. She is a recipient of the Outstanding Paper Award from the American Educational Research Association for her research in classroom assessment. Jung developed and leads the International Inclusive Leadership Program, which prepares personnel in international schools to lead inclusive efforts. Connect with her online at www.leadinclusion.org or by e-mail at ljung@sdsu.edu.

Nancy Frey is a professor of educational leadership at San Diego State University and a teacher leader at Health Sciences High & Middle College. Before joining the university faculty, Frey was a special education teacher in the Broward County (Florida) Public Schools, where she taught students at the elementary and middle school levels. She later worked for the Florida Department of Education on a statewide project for supporting students with disabilities in a general education curriculum. Frey is a recipient of the Christa McAuliffe Award for Excellence in Teacher Education from the American Association of State Colleges and Universities and the Early Career Award from the Literacy Research Association. Her research interests include reading and literacy, assessment, intervention, and curriculum design. She has published many articles and books on literacy and instruction, including *Better Learning Through Structured Teaching, How to Reach the Hard to Teach,* and *All Learning Is Social and Emotional*. She can be reached at nfrey@mail.sdsu.edu.

Douglas Fisher is a professor of educational leadership at San Diego State University and a teacher leader at Health Sciences High & Middle College. He is a member of the California Reading Hall of Fame and is the recipient of a Celebrate Literacy Award from the International Reading Association, the Farmer Award for Excellence in Writing from the National Council of Teachers of English, and a Christa McAuliffe Award for Excellence in Teacher Education from the American Association of State Colleges and Universities. Fisher has published numerous articles on improving student achievement, and his books include *The Purposeful Classroom, Building Equity,* and *Intentional and Targeted Teaching*. He can be reached at dfisher@mail.sdsu.edu.

Julie Kroener is chief of human resources and relations at Health Sciences High & Middle College. Her role includes coordinating all support services for students with and without disabilities. Kroener is a credentialed special educator and administrator in California. She collaborates with a team of general educators, special educators, and parents to ensure that students with disabilities are full members of their school and community. She can be reached at jkroener@hshmc.org.

Related ASCD Resources: Inclusive Practice

At the time of publication, the following resources were available (ASCD stock numbers in parentheses):

PD Online® Courses
Inclusion: The Basics, 2nd Edition (#PD11OC121M)
Inclusion: Implementing Strategies, 2nd Edition (#PD11OC122M)

Print Products
Beyond Co-Teaching Basics: A Data-Driven No-Fail Model for Continuous Improvement by Wendy W. Murawski and Wendy W. Lochner (#118007)

Building Equity: Policies and Practices to Empower All Learners by Dominique Smith, Nancy Frey, Ian Pumpian, and Douglas Fisher (#118031)

Building on the Strengths of Students with Special Needs: How to Move Beyond Disability Labels in the Classroom by Toby Karten (#117023)

The Differentiated Classroom: Responding to the Needs of All Learners (2nd ed.) by Carol Ann Tomlinson (#108029)

Enhancing RTI: How to Ensure Success with Effective Classroom Instruction and Intervention by Douglas Fisher and Nancy Frey (#111037)

From Goals to Growth: Intervention and Support in Every Classroom by Lee Ann Jung (#118032)

Inclusion Dos, Don'ts, and Do Betters (Quick Reference Guide) by Toby J. Karten (#QRG116082)

Leading an Inclusive School: Access and Success for ALL Students by Richard A. Villa and Jacqueline S. Thousand (#116022)

Success with IEPs: Solving Five Common Implementation Challenges in the Classroom (ASCD Arias) by Vicki Caruana (#SF117047)

A Teacher's Guide to Special Education by David Bateman and Jenifer L. Cline (#116019)

Teaching in Tandem: Effective Co-Teaching in the Inclusive Classroom by Joan Blednik and Gloria Lodata Wilson (#110029)

For up-to-date information about ASCD resources, go to www.ascd.org. You can search the complete archives of *Educational Leadership* at www.ascd.org/el.

ASCD myTeachSource®
Download resources from a professional learning platform with hundreds of research-based best practices and tools for your classroom at http://myteach source.ascd.org/

For more information, send an e-mail to member@ascd.org; call 1-800-933-2723 or 703-578-9600; send a fax to 703-575-5400; or write to Information Services, ASCD, 1703 N. Beauregard St., Alexandria, VA 22311-1714 USA.

WHOLE CHILD
TENETS

1 **HEALTHY**
Each student enters school healthy and learns about and practices a healthy lifestyle.

2 **SAFE**
Each student learns in an environment that is physically and emotionally safe for students and adults.

3 **ENGAGED**
Each student is actively engaged in learning and is connected to the school and broader community.

4 **SUPPORTED**
Each student has access to personalized learning and is supported by qualified, caring adults.

5 **CHALLENGED**
Each student is challenged academically and prepared for success in college or further study and for employment and participation in a global environment.

THE WHOLE CHILD

The ASCD Whole Child approach is an effort to transition from a focus on narrowly defined academic achievement to one that promotes the long-term development and success of all children. Through this approach, ASCD supports educators, families, community members, and policymakers as they move from a vision about educating the whole child to sustainable, collaborative actions.

Your Students, My Students, Our Students relates to the **safe, engaged, supported,** and **challenged** tenets. *For more about the ASCD Whole Child approach, visit* **www.ascd.org/wholechild.**